GOD'S NEW CREATION

Jack R. Taylor

BROADMAN PRESS
Nashville, Tennessee

4250-46
0-8054-5046-7

Dewey Decimal Classification: 233
Subject headings: MAN (THEOLOGY) // COVENANTS (THEOLOGY)
Library of Congress Catalog Card Number: 87-789
Printed in the United States of America

Unless otherwise indicated, all Scripture quotations are from the King James Version of the Holy Bible.

Library of Congress Cataloging-in-Publication Data

Taylor, Jack R.
God's new creation.

1. Christian life—Baptist authors.
2. Covenants (Theology) 3. Identification (Religion)
I. Title.
BV4501.2.T277 1987 231.7'6 87-789
ISBN 0-8054-5046-7

Dedication

To *Barbara*
my second greatest gift from God
(the first being my salvation),
my source of unending encouragement,
whose child-like excitement and
unconditional love model the subject
of this volume—
GOD'S NEW CREATION!

Foreword

A Testimony: Arthur Blessitt

Sitting at Jack Taylor's kitchen table late one night I came to understand a truth that has radically empowered my life and witness around the world. This truth was that because of Christ's death, burial, and resurrection I have a new bloodline, a new identity. The reproach of Adam and the heritage of Satan have been removed, and my nature is the nature of the indwelling Christ. This is powerful truth, whether it be in America, in the battlefields of Lebanon, or in needy South Africa. *You can be free! You can become a new creation.*

I might truly say that Jack Taylor has been my personal teacher of practical theology through the years, opening my life to truth after truth that I have had the pleasure of living out in all cultures throughout the world. This book contains truth that will release you to bold and joyful living. To every seeker of liberation, welcome to *GOD'S NEW CREATION!* Because of what happened at the cross, Satan's legal right to your life has been rendered null and void, and you are now the property of God with all legal rights and privileges to live the life that is from above.

This book will enlighten you as to your legal bill of rights as a new-creation person. The last chapter of this book is an explosion of unaltered biblical truth that should be constantly on the lips of all who know themselves to be *God's New Creations.*

THEREFORE IF ANY MAN BE IN CHRIST, HE IS
A NEW CREATURE:
OLD THINGS ARE PASSED AWAY;
BEHOLD, ALL THINGS ARE BECOME
NEW.
(2 Corinthians 5:17)

FOR IN CHRIST JESUS NEITHER CIRCUMCISION
AVAILETH ANYTHING,
NOR UNCIRCUMCISION . . .
BUT *A NEW CREATURE.*
(Galatians 6:15)

FOR WE ARE HIS WORKMANSHIP, *CREATED IN*
CHRIST JESUS . . .
UNTO GOOD WORKS,
WHICH GOD HATH BEFORE ORDAINED
THAT WE
SHOULD WALK IN THEM.
(Ephesians 2:10)

Contents

Retrospective

Would you grant an indulgence to a "man getting older"? (I am still having trouble referring to myself as "an old man," even though I do get mail from the AARP, American Association of Retired Persons!) I want to engage in some *retrospection.* This is defined in the dictionary as "the act of looking back on things past." The same dictionary also says, "Old people often enjoy retrospection." (Wish I hadn't read that!)

Well, anyway, I want to look back across the past few years of my life as an author. I am often asked, "How does one become an author?" Wish I knew! I only know how, by the grace of God, I became one.

In 1971, in the blazing heat of personal and church revival, my first book, *The Key to Triumphant Living,* was born. Someday I will tell the whole story, but let me abbreviate it here. In February of that year I was scheduled to share a testimony of revival with an interdenominational group near Nashville, Tennessee. A private plane was sent for my wife and me whose pilot had most of his experience crop-dusting! On an impulse I invited a lawyer friend along who happened to be an expert pilot. Encountering a snowstorm in the night, we were able successfully to abort the journey only through the combined expertise of both pilots and land in Little Rock, Arkansas. One delay after another eventuated in my being very late for the meeting at which I was to speak.

As the plane landed on the Nashville runway with gigantic

mounds of snow piled on either side, the Lord whispered something to my heart that I was not to understand until later. He simply mentioned a familiar place, a place I was not scheduled to be at all during that week. Upon leaving the plane I was informed by the waiting parties that the meeting where I was scheduled to speak had been cancelled due to the most severe snow storm in a decade. It was then I remembered a statement I had made under my breath while frantically trying to catch a commercial plane from Little Rock to Nashville. (I had left the other members of my party with the private plane to come on when they could.) The statement was, "Now, Lord, You have never once led me on a 'wild goose chase,' and I don't expect this to be one."

Would you believe that in minutes I was in a car headed for the place the Lord had mentioned to my heart as the plane was landing? (The Baptist Sunday School Board of the Southern Baptist Convention!) There in a prayer meeting in the prayer chapel a series of serendipities began to occur which climaxed with Broadman Press commissioning me to go home and write a book.

What a week! There were more prayer meetings, personal interviews, talk-back sessions, and ultimately a joint-committee of research and marketing people. After sharing my testimony a member of the Broadman team informed me that I should write a book. To my shock and surprise, in a few days a contract was in my hands, and a deadline of six weeks hence was given. When the shock somewhat subsided and I came to what senses I had, I faced the impossible task! By the goodness and grace of God the manuscript was finished and delivered a week early! That's how I became an author.

And now, nine books later (this being the tenth), here we go again. Across more than a decade and a half my books have sketched a map of my own personal journey. They expose the deepest workings of God in my own life. A short time after *The Key to Triumphant Living,* its sequel *Much More* was born, a simple attempt to move into the implications of the Gospel as it relates to the saved. Then followed *One Home Under God,* an elementary report of God's workings in our home. Next was *Victory Over the Devil,* a primer on spiritual warfare. Then there was *After the Spirit Comes* and a plea for balance and follow-through for those of us who were asking, "Where to from here?"

Subsequently, through the dealings of God in my own family's economy, I wrote *God's Miraculous Plan of Economy.* And then, as God began to move within my own personal prayer disciplines, I offered *Prayer: Life's Limitless Reach.* Then arrived the most difficult book I ever wrote, *What Every Husband Should Know.* (It took a whole year to write while a battle fiercely raged within me and in our home!) Finally, born in the unexpected parenthesis of an interim pastorate, I birthed *The Hallelujah Factor,* the most pleasant experience I have had as an author. And now here is *God's New Creation,* born in what I pray is the post-mid-life-crisis era of my life. (I surely don't want to go through that again!) I want this one to be a book for all seasons and passages in life, a challenge for the young, a chart for the middle years, and a companion for the aging.

Thank you for indulging me these beginning pages. You have helped me by reading. Now that I have done it I may have forgotten why I wanted to, but what difference does it make?

Oh, yes, now I remember—it was to thank you, the readers, by now into the hundreds of thousands, for your determination to "stay with me" across the years. And, yes, to Broadman Press, my publishers, and the whole Broadman team which has always been helpful, fair, and cooperative, and has kept on jogging my mind by insisting, "It's about time for another one!"

Introduction

I set out to write this book four years ago. The project was sidetracked by *The Hallelujah Factor,* my book on praise. In retrospect I was somewhat mystified at an almost sudden change in directions but, without questioning, I went joyously on my way studying and preaching on the all-important subjects of *praise* and *worship.* But in my mind, on a "back burner" as it were, there lay ever warm and warming the contents of this volume. I always knew it had to be done, and somehow knew that I for one (hopefully among others) would need to do it.

And in the providence of God the book that has been long simmering in my wife, Barbara's, heart is now ready for release. God knew, as usual, what we didn't, that the two books needed to be released together. Hers is entitled *From Rejection to Acceptance* and deals with the testimony of a struggle through rejection to find ultimate acceptance in the glorious truths surrounding her identification with Jesus Christ.

You will discover, as you read our two books, that they fit. My suggestion is that you read Barbara's book first. You will find it rather easy reading like an adventure novel. Then, when you have finished laughing and crying with her, pick this one up again and proceed slowly and cautiously. If there are statements which call for question, pause and ponder before going on. Where Scripture and references are given, take time to read them and then meditate on them. You will find this reading to be slower, calling for greater deliberation and, in some cases, some serious questioning. I not only expect that—I encourage it. These observations have long been soaking in my soul. I am absolutely convinced that, as much as these truths about our essential identity as believers in Jesus Christ were needed several years ago, the need for them at this moment is even more evidential.

"Who am I anyway?" is a question that people, secular and religious, have asked in every age with a seeming growth of intensity with passing history. And they keep coming up with different, drastic, and disappointing answers which continue to spell out one theme—d-e-s-p-a-i-r! An authentic sense of identity is not merely a luxury for an elite class of special thinkers but a necessity for all of us. If we have no sense of identity we have no sense of direction, no sense of worth, and no sense of purpose. How we view ourselves will color virtually every relationship in our lives.

In the midst of a proliferation of "self-cults," positive-thinking movements, and "pop theology," we are all wondering where we should put our landing wheels down. I was talking to a dear friend not long ago, and his statement, I thought, rather aptly summed up the situation. "I keep circling the field and about the time I think I am ready to land, someone moves the runway!"

Amid all of these the question may be asked, "Am I even allowed to believe I should ever expect to feel good about who I am?" Good question. And as much as I regret to admit it, as far as the occupants of planet earth are concerning, the jury is still out. *The thesis of this book is a resounding yes to that question. Indeed we not only have the* right *but also the* responsibility *of feeling good about who we are—if we are in Christ!*

In the pages to follow I will make an attempt to develop a *theology of identity* in down-to-earth and understandable terms. I do this with certain fear and trembling and with the realization that I have embarked upon an adventure similar to rambling across a mine field. On the one hand I will run the risk of being accused of moving too close to the dangerous doctrine of "perfectionism," and on the other hand may raise the ire of positive thinkers about some *positively negative* issues. I may even make subject matter for the next book on aberrant theology. It's not that I don't have enough problems of my own to occupy me! It's just that I sense that someone needs to sound some notes of hope and help amid a cacophony of confusion. I pray that this is the case as you read on.

I want you to sense, as we begin this study, that the Father in heaven must surely feel the same sentiments toward you that He voiced in another day to other people, "*For I know the thoughts that I think toward you, thoughts of peace, and not of evil, to give you an expected end*" (Jer. 29:11).

It is toward a satisfying and productive sense of identity, both for you as an individual and for the Body of Christ as a whole, that this volume is dedicated. May His Holy Spirit cause you to see yourself through God's eyes as . . .

GOD'S NEW CREATION.

Jack R. Taylor

1
Let's Take Up the Shake-up!

The demand for a clear sense of personal identity is never any clearer than in seasons of turbulence. The refuge available in God is never more welcomed than when the very foundations of the earth are being shaken. We are surely in one of those seasons currently. The Psalms have never offered me more comfort, solace, and certainty as in these present days. I read this very day in my Bible reading the searching question, "If the foundations be destroyed, what can the righteous do?" (Ps. 11:3).

One of the most important things the righteous can do is find out *who* and *whose* we are! It should help for us to briefly discuss the present shake-up that is taking place across the world.

A passage of Scripture in Hebrews 12:25-29 will prove pertinent here:

> See that ye refuse not him that speaketh. For if they escaped not who refused him that spake on earth, much more shall not we escape, if we turn away from him that speaketh from heaven. Whose voice then shook the earth; but now hath he promised, saying, Yet once more I shake not the earth only, but also heaven. And this word, Yet once more, signifieth the removing of those things that are shaken, as of things that are made, that those things which cannot be shaken may remain. Wherefore we receiving a kingdom which cannot be moved, let us have grace, whereby we may serve God acceptably with reverence and godly fear: FOR OUR GOD IS A CONSUMING FIRE"

That promised shaking has apparently begun! If not it is surely one of the "cautioning tremors" preceding it. A dear friend of mine calls it "the shakings of awakening."

Let me make some observations about such shakings as described here in this passage.

First, the Shaking Is *Predictable*

We really shouldn't be surprised. God has *promised* such shakings. Jesus made clear that "in the world ye shall have tribulation" (John 16:33*b*).

History has *portrayed* such shakings. Every man and woman whose biography is touched upon in biblical history endured times of fierce shakings. Time would fail to tell about even a few of them. In the history of the church the same is true. Thousands have languished in prison, endured hardships, and had their lives abruptly ended because of their faith. And the rumblings have never ceased.

Then, personal testimony *proves* the predictability of these shakings. At this point I am not certain whether it is this season through which we are passing, my own age making me more aware, or some other unknown, but it seems there is more personal shaking than I have ever before witnessed.

Everything is being shaken! There is an obvious *economic* shaking. Nations teeter on the brink of total economic collapse, threatening to carry whole continents with them to oblivion. There are also shakings that pertain to *education.* Entire structures of our learning processes are being questioned. There are also *political* shakings all over the world. Empires are falling; revolution is fomenting.

And the shakings go on in the entire culture of mankind on earth. It is not a pretty picture from where we stand, unless we can see that "yet once more God is speaking loudly to planet earth." The significant matter here is that God is quick and direct to own the initiative. He is doing the shaking.

Second, the Shaking Is *Purposeful*

This God-induced turbulence seems to have a simple two-fold design. First, it is for the removing of the rubbish of the unreal. Earth and heaven are being shaken until everything that is shakable is removed.

> Yet once more, signifieth the removing of things that are shaken, as of things that are made . . . (Heb. 12:27*a*).

Then, secondly, the shakings will reaffirm the real.

> . . . that those things which cannot be shaken may remain (Heb. 12:27*b*).

When the rumblings have quieted, then the real will remain, and the unreal will be removed.

Third, the Shaking Is Profitable.

In times of ease and prosperity we tend to find our identities in things that are superficial, temporary, and less than ultimate in value. We will find profit in these times of difficulty because we will *discard the ungenuine and impermanent.* That will inevitably lead to the second result, namely, the *rediscovery of the real and the genuine.* We never seem to discover that God is all we *need* until one day we look around and find Him to be all we *have!*

The great profit of this shaking is summarized in these words: "Wherefore receiving a kingdom which cannot be removed . . ."

That is ultimate blessing, receiving an unmoveable kingdom! Imagine it—a kingdom which cannot be shaken! Where is it? What is it? Those great kingdoms, once declared immoveable, Babylon, Egypt, Rome, Assyria, Greece, are gone! Health is moveable and fleeting. Wealth is not a lasting kingdom. The visible church is moveable. Denominations are temporary. Institutions are not here to stay. And yet, we have received a kingdom which cannot be moved. Where have we now arrived? At the fountainhead of our essential identity, our citizenship in the *eternal kingdom.*

We cannot afford to find our identity in wealth; it is fleeting. We must not connect our identity with power; it is fickle. We dare not tie our identity to beauty or youth; they will leave us slowly or suddenly. We will regret it if we find identity even in the furnishings of our religious life, forms, organizations, or denominations. They, too, will prove shakeable.

If we are deceived into finding our essential identity in any of these "moveables," when they are taken we will have lost the basic ingredient of life. I view this very issue in people today losing their wealth, and with it their reason for living, because they found their sense of identity in it. If we have discovered our identity in our citizenship in the immovable kingdom we will be "shaken into stability."

Before we leave this passage in Hebrews let us see . . .

Fourth, the Shaking Brings a *Proposal*

We have been informed that we have received a kingdom which cannot be moved. We have found the one fixed thing in life, the Kingdom, ruled by the King, of which we who are saved are eternal citizens. How then shall we live? Here is the brief and pointed answer: "Let us have grace, whereby we may serve God acceptably with reverence and godly fear" (Heb. 12:28*b*)

Here is the proposal to the shaken. First, we are to adopt a stance of grace and gratitude. Second, we are to worship God. The word used in the original for "serve" is latrueo which, when used in relationship to God, means "worship." This worship is to be characterized by a determination to please, reverence, and exercise godly fear.

God . . . a Consuming Fire!

With this mysterious statement the twelfth chapter of Hebrews closes. Fire is a contradiction. It may be a feared foe or faithful friend, a useful ally or awful alien. The same is true of our God. The statement, "Our God is a consuming fire," brings tremendous comfort to those on one side of God but dreadful alarm and consternation to those on the other side. As a fire He cleanses and cauterizes or condemns and consumes.

When God led the Israelites out of Egypt he went before them by day in a pillar of cloud and by night in a pillar of fire. They were poised on the shores of the Red Sea across which they would exit the bondage of Egypt. Pharaoh sent his chariots and would have massacred the entire race had it not been for one factor, the presence of God in the cloud and fire! Listen to the narrative in Exodus 14:19-20:

> And the angel of God, which went before the camp of Israel, removed and went behind them; and the pillar of the cloud went from before their face, stood behind them: And it came between the camp of the Egyptians and the camp of Israel; *and it was a cloud of darkness to them but it gave light by night to these:* so that the one came not near the other all the night

From the Egyptian side it was darkness; from the side of Israel it was light. In essence, then, I emphasize that what God is to you is determined by your essential identify.

Can we not establish, then, from the outset that the whole design of the shaking around us, as well as within us, is bringing us to see who God is and who we are?

2
Our Covenant God

The overriding preoccupation of the Scriptures is to answer the question, "How can sinful man ever be properly related to Holy God?" It is also patently clear that this is the preoccupation of every religion on the face of the earth. Sin may be defined variously, and the gods of these religions called different names, but the general idea is the same: How can man in his condition have fellowship and relationship with "whoever" is out there?

If we are to reach a sense of authentic identity we must accept as foundational the demand that we come to know what God is like, what He has said about Himself, and how we proposes to bridge the gap between Himself as holy and man as unholy. This is the fundamental question to which all theology addresses itself—the God-man relationship. How does God relate to man? How can man establish a relationship with God? Is man God's pawn who has absolutely no voice in his ultimate destiny? Can there be any real stability, dependability, or predictability to this one-sided relationship of the infinite, perfect God with the finite, sinful man?

The answer to these searching questions which have to do with all of us is found in one word, *COVENANT*. The idea of covenant is not only preeminent in Scripture, it is *pervasive* there. That is, all Scripture is bound within the framework of a covenant.

It is absolutely essential that we recognize that whatever our identity—and thus our purpose and destiny—involves, it will have everything to do with covenant. And with that recognition there comes a fundamental assumption that whatever can be known of God, His disposition, His design for life on earth, and His dealings with mankind is best understood by an acquaintance with the concept of covenant. In summary, we are dealing with a covenant God Who, in His sovereignty, has chosen to do what He does within the context of a covenant.

Spurgeon declared, "All God's dealings with man have a covenant character. It hath so pleased Him to arrange it, that He will not deal with us except through a covenant, nor can we deal with Him except in the same manner. Adam in the garden was under a covenant with God, and God was in covenant with him." In a glorious message, "The Blood of the Everlasting Covenant," Spurgeon makes crystal clear his conviction that the relationship between earth and heaven centers on covenant. He continued, "It is important, then, since the covenant is the only ladder which reaches from earth to heaven . . . since it is the only way in which God has intercourse with us, and by which we can deal with Him, that we should know how to discriminate between covenant and covenant; and should not be in any darkness or error with regard to what is the covenant of grace, and what is not."[2]

Since, then, we have asserted that the covenant forms the entrance to all we may know about God, and thus about us, we will not begrudge the time and space used to discuss both the *Covenant God and His Covenant.*

Because God is the Creator and the covenant was created by Him, we will look first at this God through and in Whom we discover our true identity. This study will land us squarely in the discovery of the identity for which all mankind longs. We will learn that we are children of an immoveable kingdom because we are children of an eternal covenant.

We will leave the discussion of the covenant's nature to a later chapter, but it is vital to know that the means we use to distinguish the two divisions of our Bible, namely "Old and New Testaments," could properly be termed "Old and New

Covenants." Thus, we observe that no part of Holy Scripture is excluded from covenant implications.

All we know of God for certain has come to us through a covenant, for that is how He has chosen to relate Himself to mankind. We have no question or choice in the matter, nor should we desire such, for God's choice of methods in dealing with us has given us such advantages we could not possibly hope to better ourselves, though we had a thousand years to study and arrange our case.

Realizing, then, that we know covenant through God, and God through covenant, let us observe several vital premises about this God of Covenant.

This Covenant God Took the Initiative

Our Bible appropriately begins with "In the beginning God . . . ." This whole affair of human history was all God's idea! He took the initiative; He created the world and humanity according His own good pleasure. It is vital we believe in the accuracy and reliability of the Genesis record because that is the wellspring from which most of what we believe about God issues. If that is flawed, then our knowledge of God is flawed, and all that is left for us is a flawed identity. Without accurate knowledge of the roots from which we have sprung and of the God Whose hand has created us, we have no hope of arriving at a satisfying sense of who we are or why we exist.

This all-important factor of *initiative* should be kept in mind here. God took the initiative because He, and He alone, had the right of initiative. And He retains that right through time and eternity. Failure to accept this fact as basic, and to consent that it is both valid and right, will likely result in an elevated respect for our own intelligence to such an extent that we will call into question all divinely-revealed truth.

This divine initiative from eternity past through enternity future is included in the attribute of sovereignty, that attribute of God which describes Him as self-determining in His actions and absolute in His power. He answers to no one but Himself and seeks His own good pleasure.

In this disposition our Covenant God came to Adam in Genesis 3, to Noah in Genesis 9, and to Abraham in Genesis 12, 13, 15, and 17. That same disposition dictated His approach to Moses in Exodus 20 and to David in 2 Samuel 7.

This Covenant God Dictates the Terms of Covenant

Sovereignty in initiative gives way to sovereignty in the meditation of the covenant. This simply means that we are what we are on the basis of God's sovereignty. We have the rights we have on the same basis. The terms of the covenant not only reflected God's pursuit of His Own purpose but a revelation of his purpose in relating to mankind.

When Abram was ninety-nine years old God came to him and introduced Himself as "the Almighty God." The Hebrew name here is *El Shaddai.* We will look at the significance of that name later in the chapter. For now it will suffice to say the name asserted that God was "all-sufficient." God was in effect stating "Abram, I am ALMIGHTY, and that means I enable what I command and can pay for what I order!"

That self-determining facet of our covenant God is never any clearer than when he is clarifying the terms of covenant. In Genesis 17 there are fourteen "I wills," seven of them connected to the covenant terms pertaining to Abram and seven, to Sarai.

I am sure that poor, bewildered Abraham (his new covenant name) was by now reeling in dismay and drowning in questions. After being informed that he would be a "father of many nations" and that Sarah (her new covenant name) would be a "mother of nations," Abraham must have thought he had heard it all wrong and that Ishmael, his already-existing son by Hagar, was who God had in mind. Abraham exclaimed, "Shall a child be born unto him that is an hundred years old? and shall Sarah, that is ninety years old, bear?" (Gen. 17:17*b*)

God's answer was patently, "Sarah thy wife shall bear thee a son indeed; and thou shalt call his name Isaac: and I will establish my covenant with him for an everlasting covenant, and with his seed after him" (Gen. 17:19).

What was happening here between God and Abraham was because of what had happened in Genesis 15:18, "In the same day the Lord made a covenant with Abram."

Thus we see clearly that the covenant God not only takes the initiative but dictates the terms of covenant.

This Covenant God Mediates the Terms of Covenant

Moses reminded the people in Deuteronomy 7:9, "Know therefore that the Lord, thy God, He is God, the faithful God, which keepeth covenant with them that love him and keep his commandments."

The word *berith* which we will discuss later is found 300 times in the Old Testament and is translated "covenant." Some of those references are in the Book of Leviticus where we view God revealing His mediating work in covenant relationships. We find such statements as:

> So I will turn toward you and make you fruitful and multiply you, and I will *confirm* my convenant with you (Lev. 26:9).
>
> I will bring upon you a sword which will execute vengeance for the covenant . . . (26:25).
>
> . . . then I will remember my covenant with Jacob . . . with Isaac . . . and Abraham . . . and I will remember the land (26:42).
>
> But I will remember for them the covenant with their ancestors, whom I brought out of the land of Egypt in the sight of the nations, that I might be their God. I am the Lord (26:45).

These and other passages make it clear that God stays

around to mediate what he initiates. He remembers, confirms, and executes judgment on the basis of covenant.

Moses revealed his knowledge of the covenantal nature of Israel's relationship with God when he declared to the people:

> And he declared unto you his covenant, which he commanded you to perform, even ten commandments; And he wrote them upon two tables of stone (Deut. 4:13).
>
> Take heed to yourselves, lest ye forget the covenant of the Lord your God, which he made with you . . . (Deut. 4:23).
>
> (For the Lord thy God is a merciful God:) he will not forsake thee, neither destroy thee, nor forget the covenant of thy fathers which he sware unto them (4:31)."

These and many other Scriptures serve to support our claim that our covenant God remains faithful to maintain the terms of His covenant. We will hear him over and over making statements such as:

> For I have made a covenant with thy chosen . . .
>
> My mercy will I keep for him for evermore, and my covenant shall stand fast with him.
>
> My covenant will I not break, nor alter the thing that is gone out of my lips (Psalm 89:3, 28, 34).

This Covenant God Has Covenant Names

The fact is that all God's names reflect covenant character. He is *Jehovah* as is indicated in some 6,823 times in the Old Testament. This name is derived from the Hebrew verb of being, *havah.* The Hebrew word *chavah* is strikingly similar to it and means "living" or "life." The connection is obvious as we meet the God of the Bible who is both "being" and "life," the self-existent One. He is Who He is! He need be no more than He is. He is no less than He is. He depends upon no one outside Himself to be what or Who He is! He always has been Who He is and will always be Who He is! He is the only one who has always been able to say what He said to Moses, "I am that I am . . ." (Ex. 3:14*a*). He has always been I AM; He will always be I AM; and He is now at this moment I AM!

Now, the reason I am making much of this fact about God is: *His identity is fixed, permanent, and unchangeable.* It is from Who He is that you and I derive our own identities. As we discover our identities in Who He is, our identities are as permanent as His.

I am particularly intrigued with what are generally called the "compound Jehovah names." They are also called the *redemptive* names of God. I prefer to call them *God's covenant names* because I believe them to be, in fact, a special revelation of his covenantal behavior and relationships. Most of them arise out of some historic episode and reflect some character trait revealed through that incident in Jehovah as contrasted to false gods and as sufficient for every human need.

Let's briefly look at each of those eight covenant names for our covenant God:

JEHOVAH-JIREH

Abraham was ordered to take Issac to Mount Moriah and offer him as a burnt offering. Because he understand covenant Abraham, dutifully and without question he set out to obey his covenant God. Just as he was about to take the life of his own son, the angel stayed his hand, informed him that he had passed the test, and pointed to a ram caught in the thicket, ready to be the sacrifice instead of Isaac. In Genesis 22:14, Abraham joyously called the name of that place "Jehovah-Jireh: as it is said to this day, In the mount of the Lord it will be seen." The Hebrew word *jireh* means "to see." God is the one who sees everything and *sees to* everything. This is the name for God as *Provider.* It is an interesting play on words to note that the English word is derived from two Latin words, "pro," meaning "before" and "vida," meaning "to see." Thus provision is simply the ability to see beforehand and to see to what is seen!

JEHOVAH-ROPHE (RAPHA)

As God was leading His covenant people through the wilderness He revealed Himself in Exodus 15:17 as their *Healer.* He promised them that if they would listen to Him, hearken to His words, and do what He said, he would allow none of the diseases found among the Egyptians to come upon them. He then announced, "For I am the Lord that healeth thee" (Ex. 15:17). In essence He was revealing, "I am the Lord Who keeps you well!"

Can you see the marvelous manner in which the covenant God is revealing Himself through His covenant names?

JEHOVAH-NISSI

Warfare, then and now, is inevitable. Words that cause us all to reflect are found in Exodus 17:8, "Then came Amalek . . ." This grandson of Esau has living kin all around us today! About the time we start to do well spiritually, it happens, "Then came Amalek!" But our covenant God is also a God of war. After Joshua had soundly trounced Amalek in the Valley of Rephidim, God told him to write it "for a memorial in a book" (Ex. 17:14*a*). It was then that Moses built an altar and called the place Jehovah-Nissi. Nissi is a word that means, among other things, "to glisten." It is also translated "pole," "standard," or "ensign." They were celebrating God's covenant character revealed in His being their standard of victory.

JEHOVAH-M'KADESH

This name is found in Leviticus 20:8 where God says, "And ye shall keep my statutes, and do them: I am the Lord Who sanctifies you." When God makes covenant with man, inherent in that covenant is separation. This word "sanctify" means "to hallow," "to consecrate," or "to dedicate." It is sobering on the one hand that this covenant God demands that we be holy and assuring on the other hand that He is *Jehovah-M'Kadesh* who makes us holy!

JEHOVAH-SHALOM

How encouraging as we come to view the identity of Him with Whom we are in covenant! As these names are found in the Scriptures there is a beautiful progression of revelation as to Who He is. In Judges 6:24 we read, "Then Gideon built an altar there unto the Lord, and called it Jehovah-Shalom." He was declaring, "My God is my Peace!" You will remember that Gideon lived in an era of intense judgment upon Israel. God had delivered them into the hands of the Midianites. The times in which Gideon lived were everything but peaceful. The fierce Midianites constantly harrassed the Israelites, encamping against them, destroying their crops, and leaving no sustenance for their survival. During this era Gideon was stealthily threshing wheat by a winepress, hoping against hope that he could successfully complete the task before the enemy came to destroy it.

An angel sat under an oak tree nearby and saluted Gideon with the words, "The Lord is with thee, thou mighty man of valor." In the ensuing conversation the cautious Gideon insisted that there be some proof that this creature was genuine. He went to prepare a goat and unleavened cakes of flour and brought these as a sacrifice. The angel responded by touching the sacrifice with the end of his staff, and the whole sacrifice suddenly ignited and burned to a crisp. Gideon was left in fright as the angel vanished. But the Lord spoke, "Peace be unto you; fear not; thou shalt not die." In the midst of fear and panic Gideon found God as a God of peace!

JEHOVAH-ROHI

This is the designation found in Psalm 23 and simply means "shepherd" or "guide." What a comforting thought! The God Who initiates covenant is also the One who guides the covenant people in all the details of covenant living! The Psalmist, in Psalm 80:1, called God, "O Shepherd of Israel, thou that leadest Joseph like a flock; thou that dwellest between the cherubim, shine forth."

Isaiah wrote of God, "He shall feed His flock like a shepherd; he shall gather the lambs with His arm, and carry them in His bosom, and shall gently lead those that are young" (40:11-12).

Of course, one of the greatest possible considerations from this name of God is: He is not just the Shepherd, but He is *my* Shepherd!

JEHOVAH-TSIDKENU

We move on in the descriptions of the character of our covenant God. In Jeremiah 23:6 is this designation, "In His days Judah will be saved, and Israel shall dwell safely; and this is the name whereby He shall be called, THE LORD OUR RIGHTEOUSNESS." The word *tsidkenu* is derived from *tsedek* which originally meant "straight" or "stiff." We are informed constantly that God is righteous and deals with people righteously. "But the Lord shall endure forever; He hath prepared His throne for judgement. And He shall judge the world in righteousness, He shall minister judgement in uprightness (Ps. 9:7-8)

Since God is the perfectly righteous One he administers the covenant in righteousness, demanding righteousness on the one hand and providing righteousness on the other.

JEHOVAH-SHAMMAH

We round out this series of God's names with the one that crowns the whole. The last statement of the Book of Ezekiel (48:35). This name literally means, "God is there!" How fitting a climax to the covenant descriptions of the God who mediates our covenant! He is there, always there, tending to the covenant children.

The Jews always held this name to have literal significance. They believed it to mean that God would literally come down and dwell with His people. Thus, when it was announced that the name of the Messiah would be "Immanuel" (God with us) there was special fulfilment.

And He has promised us, "For where two or three are gathered together in my name, there am I in the midst of them" (Matt. 18:20).

We see in these eight names for God a perfect provision for our identity. We are who we are because of Who He is and because of what He, through covenant, is making of us. We should be reminded:

God is Who He says He is.
I am who God says I am.
God can do what He says He can do.
I can do what God says I can do.
God has what He says He has.
I have what God says I have.

Andrew Murray, in his splendid classic, *The Two Covenants*, "Blessed is the man who truly knows God as his Covenant God; who knows what the covenant promises him; what unwavering confidence of expectation it secures, that all its terms will be fulfilled in him; what a claim and hold it gives on the Covenant-keeping God Himself."[3]

THIS COVENANT GOD IS REVEALED AS *FATHER*

It would border on travesty to omit the most significant name for God in the Bible. The significance of Jesus is as the *Son of God.* He teaches us that we who are His children can address God as "Father." Whatever the covenant is perceived to be, its meaning is enhances as we come to realize we are not only in personal covenant with Father, but we are part of a Covenant Family. Within that family, not in isolation, the full significance of the covenant can be realized here on earth.

Here I feel that we have cleared away the rubbish and have laid down a foundation for a basic understanding of our essential identity. In seeking an elementary understanding of Who our God really is, we have found His nature and names as windows through which to view the very face and heart of God. We shall in the next chapter view the glorious covenant as the very foundation for erecting a valid identity for ourselves as individuals and for redeemed humanity as a whole.

3
The Nature of Covenant

I am compelled to remind you that, though we are looking at the matter of covenant, we do so to arrive at a secure and satisfying sense of identity as believers in Jesus Christ.

For that reason there will be no need to cover exhaustively the matter of covenant. However, a working knowledge of the subject, as it pervades the Bible, seems almost indispensable to the study of who we are as a people of God. I considered the matter so important that my first proposal for this book's title was *New Covenant—New Creation.* I am asking for the reader to be patient through these pages as we lay a foundation for a fuller understanding of the "deal we have with God," as well as the God with Whom we deal.

In what is recognized as the classic work on the matter of covenant, H. Clay Trumbull in his book, *The Blood Covenant* documents to a satisfying degree the fact that all blood covenants are derivatives of biblical covenants. He is not alone in this valid conclusion. K. M. Campbell, in *God's Covenant,* wrote: "We must remember that the covenant was not an idea invented by pagan societies. A covenant was entered into by God and Adam, and we believe that just as all ancient civilizations retain garbled versions of the true stories of the fall, the flood, and other historical truths contained in the Scripture, so the conscience of the pagan world retained the notion of covenant."

So, I am claiming here that a familiarity with the matter of covenant in general, and of the Old Covenant (Testament) and the New Covenant (Testament) in particular, is necessary to and supportive of a satisfying understanding of our essential identity as members of the Body of Christ. However, a word of caution seems appropriate. As intriguing as the study of covenant always seems to be, we should not become bogged down with the interesting details of it and forget the object of our search in the first place, namely, discovering identity.

The grand, unifying principle in the Bible is the divine-human relationship as it issues from the covenants between God and man. It is no exaggeration, then, to conclude that covenantal theology is at the root of all biblical thinking. We must consider seriously the claim that all theology rises out of covenants. The covenants, in biblical terms, spell out God's condescension to man, affecting man's salvation.

Malcolm Smith, in his book *Blood Brothers in Christ,* makes this claim, "We cannot avoid the blood covenant. It faces us either directly or by implication in every story and miracle in the Scriptures. Any hope that we have of salvation can only be understood inside the framework of the covenant. On what basis does a sinful man hope to approach God and find acceptance with Him? What audacity puts into our heads the idea that we may pray and receive an answer? Without a solid foundation faith becomes nothing more than a pathetic presumption, a faith in faith which is a leap into meaninglessness. Biblical faith is a response to something God has done. God lays the foundation, takes the initiative, and faith is but man's response to that. There is a solid foundation on which every promise and hope of salvation lies, against which every threat and warning becomes vividly real. *That foundation is the blood covenant.*"[1]

Andrew Murray received a letter in which a friend testified to what he was learning about intercessory prayer as it was enhanced by a knowledge of covenant truths. He summed up his convictions at the end of the letter by remarking, "If you would take the covenant and speak of it as God would enable you to speak, I think that would be the quickest way the Lord could take to make His Church wake up to the power He has placed into our hands in giving us a Covenant. I would be glad if you would tell God's people that they have a covenant."[2]

It will prove, in my estimation, a life-altering experience to relate the implications of biblical covenant, not only to our identity but to every exercise of our faith. With that in mind, let us move on with expectation.

Covenant Definitions

Kittel, in his *Theological Dictionary of the New Testament,* notes, "Attempts to derive the meaning of the term have not led to any clear or certain conclusions." The majority of scholars, however, seem to think that *berith* is derived from an Assyrian word which means "to bind" or "fetter." Others maintain, probably because of the accompanying ceremonies involving blood-letting, that the word means "to cut."

The Greek counterpart of the Hebrew word *berith* is *diatheke* which means "an unequal covenant," where one does all the giving and the other, all the taking. This word is found more than thirty times in the New Testament. It is believed this word has implications, in addition to the idea of a special arrangement between two parties, relating to our idea of a will or testament.

It is not difficult to see that the very definition of a covenant, however varying the shades may be, implies the connection of that covenant and the identity of the covenanting parties. In other words, once a covenant has been entered and agreed upon, the identities of the principle parties are set. We are on the right track!

Major Covenants in the Old Testament

Again, we meet disagreement in the listing of these covenants. It seems to be basically a matter of one's opinion. I prefer to list them and their qualities as follows:

ADAMIC: The only near-confirmation that the agreement God had with Adam was a covenant is found in Hosea 6:7: ". . . they [Israel] like Adam [margin] have transgressed the covenant." Even though this marginal rendering is disputed there is clear evidence that what went on between Adam and God was covenantal in nature. Some divide this one covenant into two: Edenic and Adamic. Observe the features of this covenant:

1. There were two agreeing parties: God and Adam.
2. Conditions were imposed on Adam: obedience to God's commandments, especially refraining from eating of the tree of knowledge of good and evil.
3. There was an implied promise: eternal life and immortality, represented by access to the tree of life.
4. There was a threat of death in the event of disobedience. When Adam and Eve sinned, a series of curses was invoked upon them. The word *curse* is covenantal language being associated with the penalty of breaking a covenant.

The seriousness of that covenant, and the ultimate and ongoing expenses incurred in its violation, make up much of the text of our Old Testament. God's arrangement for those expenses to be paid and the damage repaired make up the remainder of the biblical text in the New Testament. Among the devastating effects of violating that first covenant is that of *lost identity* on the part of Adam and Eve, an identity which was not to be fully recovered until the coming of Christ.

NOAHIC: This covenant was made with Noah just before God destroyed the earth with the great Flood: ". . . Noah found grace in the eyes of the Lord . . . and God said to Noah, The end of all flesh is come before Me; for the earth is filled with violence through them; and behold, I will destroy them with the earth . . . *But with thee will I establish my Covenant*" (Gen. 6:8, 13, 18). What are the features of this covenant?

1. Again, God took the initiative, knowing what He was about to do.

2. The covenant was primarily made with Noah.
3. However, many were benefited from it who were not in on its origin.
5. It was a covenant of preservation.

We may find consolation that many, even those in the sinful world, benefit from God's covenants with his children.

ABRAHAMIC: I have previously made reference to this covenant. It was made with Abraham when he was seventy-five years old in Genesis 15 and renewed when he was ninety-nine in Genesis 17. Its principal features are:

1. He would be the father of many nations.
2. His name would be changed.
3. He would be fruitful, and nations and kings would come to him.
4. The covenant would be established with him and his progeny.
5. The land of Canaan would be given as an inheritance.
6. Every male would be circumcised.
7. Every male baby would be circumcised.
8. Sarai's name would be changed.
9. Isaac would the child of the covenant.

It is significant that in Exodus 2:24 it is said, "And God heard their groaning, and *God remembered His covenant* with Abraham, with Isaac, and with Jacob." It is further stated that he looked upon them and had respect unto them. Their identity as covenant offspring was the key factor in their subsequent deliverance.

SINIATIC: This was the most important Old Testament covenant and was made between God and Israel represented by Moses. This covenant was the foundation of Israel's relationship with God and colored their whole history as God's chosen people. Here are its principal features:

1. It was written in tables of stone by God.
2. It was specific and binding.

3. The laws written would regulate the relationship between the Israelites and God.

More than any recorded covenant in the Old Testament, this one points up the legal (lawful) nature of such a covenant relationship.

DAVIDIC: This covenant is recorded in 2 Samuel 7:12-14: ". . . I will set up thy seed after thee, which shall proceed out of thy bowels, and I will establish his kingdom. He shall build a house for My name, and I will establish the throne of his kingdom forever. I will be his Father and he shall be my son." Its features include:

1. It was wholly promissory.
2. It carried human obligation.
3. It reached beyond the immediate temporal to the ultimate in Christ.

As we leave the principal covenants of the Old Testament, it is good to keep in mind that when God spoke of covenant he always spoke in the singular. This has one overpowering implication: *that as God views the whole matter of covenant he sees all expressions of such as one eternal arrangement which climaxes in the New Covenant sealed with the blood of Jesus Christ.* God has one covenant in mind, a covenant which He renews to different people at different stages of the history of salvation. I will save a discussion of the New Covenant until a later chapter.

Covenant Illustrations

We may learn much and benefit immensely from a study of several covenant illustrations in the Bible, as well as from other sources.

In no one place do we have the details of the ceremonies that accompanied the cutting of a covenant. In the case with Abraham, God commanded that Abraham take a heifer, a goat, and a ram, all three years old, as well as a turtledove and a pigeon.

Abraham cut the animals in half but did not divide the birds. When the sun went down a "smoking furnace and a burning lamp passed between those pieces" (Gen. 15:17). It is assumed here that a Covenant Representative, a proxy as God's agent, walked between the bloody havles of the animals to validate the covenant between God and Abraham. In later versions of this ceremony the two parties would slaughter the animal or animals, cut them in half, and walk in a figure eight in and around them. They would then stand with their backs to the bloody halves, facing each other, and make their vows of faithfulness in the covenant relationship. One of the significances of standing between those bloody halves was what the covenanting parties said after that, "God so do to you and me if we break the terms of this covenant" (referring to the dividing in half of the animal).

In later days and other versions of the covenant, different facets were added to the ceremony, such as the taking off of a garment and handing it to the contracting party, the changing or combination of names, cutting parts of the body (wrist or leg), mixing of blood, drinking or a portion from a common cup, the setting up of a covenant memorial, the planting of a tree, and the sharing together of a common covenant meal.

Many of the matters we take for granted in our culture had their roots and origins in covenants. The changing of the name of the bride in marriage has undeniable covenant roots. The simple handshake is a part of the covenant ceremony. The raising of the hand to take a vow is derived from covenant ceremonies.

We have, in my estimation, abundant reason to believe that Trumbull, in *The Blood Covenant,* was right in his conclusion that all the primitive religions found their bases in the biblical idea of blood covenant. It has left its marks and symbols in every culture of the world.[6]

Often, as we shall see later, the mark of the covenant was a slit on the wrist of the covenanting parties which was made more obvious by putting some foreign substance into the open wound. This would cause the desired effect of making the scar more obvious as an easily discernible mark of covenant. Again we encournter the concept of identity as inseparably bound to covenant.

The Case of David, Jonathan, and Mephibosheth

After David had killed the Philistine giant, Goliath, with the giant's head in his hand he appeared in the presence of King Saul (1 Sam. 17:57). After David and the king had finished with the conversation, David and Jonathan entered into a covenant of strong friendship. The depth of that covenant is evidenced by what happened as described in 1 Samuel 18:4:

> And Jonathan stripped himself of the robe that was upon him, and gave it to David, and his garments, even to his sword, and to his bow, and to his girdle.

The story of the relationship of David and Jonathan is freighted with notable features of the covenant relationship suggestive of our relationship with Jesus Christ, the Mediator of the New Covenant. Perhaps the greatest significance of the David-Jonathan relationship is observed in the case of Mephibosheth, the crippled little prince.

The covenant between Jonathan and David, as most covenants do, embraced yet unborn generations. They made their vows not only to each other but to unborn children. Subsequent offspring would be born "in" covenant as David and Jonathan were to each other. Tragic and perilous years followed in their relationship as Saul developed an insane jealousy of David. In all this Jonathan remained true to David. The blood of covenant was stronger than the blood of family. That covenant was to be tried to the limit but was honored and observed by both David and Jonathan. The story of the death of Jonathan and Saul broke the heart of David.

When the news of the death of Saul and Jonathan reached

the palace there was pandemonium. Mephibosheth was the infant son of Jonathan. His nurse had forgotten him and went back to rescue him from the royal nursery. In her haste she stumbled with the infant in her arms, which resulted in his being crippled in both legs, a paralytic for life.

This part of the royal family escaped to a desert town by the name of Lodebar, headquarters of the desert chieftan, Amiel. There Mephibosheth was raised in an atmosphere of bitterness and hostility to any thought of David the King. Surely the primitive surroundings formed the background of plots of revolution when David would be deposed and Mephibosheth could assume the throne. And so the little crippled lad grew, and with his growth the resentment and hostility grew with the determination to strike a blow at David if he ever had the chance. In poverty, paralysis, and pity Mephibosheth languished in the dusty misery of Lodebar.

David's kingdom was established in glory under him, but there lingered in him the deep love reflected and remembered in his relationship with the late Jonathan. In 2 Samuel 9:1, David asks, "Is there any left of the house of Saul, that I may show him kindness for Jonathan's sake." That question was to launch a drama like few ever told in truth or fiction.

The search for the kin of Jonathan began, and soom there was found a former servant in the house of Saul by the name of Ziba who informed David's men that there was indeed an offspring of Jonathan, a little paralytic, Mephibosheth of Lodebar. David, like God, remembered the covenant. Surely as he thought of the son of Jonathan, he thought of that dramatic day when he and Jonathan walked between the halves of the slain animals, shared their garments and weapons, spoke their covenant vows, and entered into a covenant which was to be binding in yet unborn generations. David remembered his love for Jonathan and his sadness and dismay upon hearing of his death. Now he would have the privilege of extending his unexpressed love to Jonathan, now dead, through his son, Mephibosheth.

The royal entourage was readied, the king's own regal chariot was prepared, and the search party was dispatched. Beyond imagination was the sight of the king's detachment and chariots as they rolled into the remote desert village of Lodebar and up to the shanty which crippled, pitiful Mephibosheth called home. His name was called by a royal representative, and fear struck him like lightning. But he knew, in his condition, that flight was out of the question. Perhaps with a whine, he admitted his identity, surely believing that the next event in his life would be . . . his death. But to his shock and surprise he was lifted by gentle hands and carried to the most elegant of the chariots. The softness of the royal cushions almost buried the lame lad. "Where are you taking me?" he must have queried, half in fear and half in anger. "We are going to see the king!" was the reply. A combination of fear, hate, and confusion filled the heart of the crippled boy.

After awhile the chariots arrived at their destination with their treasured freight, Mephibosheth. He was ushered into the palace and his crippled, useless legs dragged lifeless feet across royal rugs. At last *he stood before the king himself.*

One look at the king and crutches flew in both directions, Mephibosheth falling to his face in reverence to the king. David savored the name of Mephibosheth as he might have tasted the finest of gourmet foods. It must have sounded like a salute to royalty as David called Mephibosheth by name. "Behold thy servant!" was all Mephibosheth could think to mutter, his tongue seeming as large as his fist.

"Fear not" David replied, "I will show you kindness for Jonathan, your father's sake, and I will restore all the land of Saul to you, and you will eat at my table for the rest of your life." At that, an adage, best understood in Oriental cultures, escaped from the lips of the humbled little cripple, "Who am I that you would have looked upon a dead dog such as I am?" Though the record does not indicate such, my imagination compels me to believe that the great king left his throne, losing his composure, and in tears lifted the lad to his bosom, bathing his dirty face in tears.

Let your imagination finish the drama and picture the lad bathed and bright in royal garments, looking like the prince he is and has been. Perhaps, just perhaps, somewhere in the palace there is an accuser who knows Mephibosheth from Lodebar days. As the prince is carried to the sumptuous table for supper the accuser whispers, "I know who you are. You hated David. You would have killed him had you had opportunity. You have no right here in the palace!" I can feature Mephibosheth answering, "Sir, you are right on more than one count, but when we get into the presence of the king I want you to notice that scar on his right wrist. Do you know what that means? My father and David were in covenant. Everything they would ever have belonged to each other. *And that mark means I belong to David, and David is as a Father to me.*" The accuser is forever silenced and the future of Mephibosheth secured.

I have employed this story as a covenant illustration because, from many angles, it tells your story and mine. It brings to our view striking similarities to our own spiritual journey.

We once languished in Lodebar-like circumstances.

We had lost our identity and were helpless.

We wallowed in fear, pity, and confusion with the accuser lodging lies in our minds about the goodness of God.

But David's progeny, none other than the Lord Jesus Christ, came to our misery and lifted us on gentle hands to forgiveness, grace, and royalty. Our feet have been under His table ever since.

Covenant determined identity! May God help you to see it as we look further into the covenant in Chapter 4.

4
Covenant Clarifications

You and I have a tremendous advantage in being alive at this particular time in history. We have been blessed with considerable light. However, much light suggests much responsibility. We have more resources by which we may have a clear sense of identity than any age before us. Light or revelation unheeded ushers in judgment. Therefore, we must practice care and discernment to pursue, receive, and implement all the resources of revelation accessible to us.

Our Bible

The chief resource, of course, is our Bible. We accept it as a definitive statement and an accurate assessment of all about which it speaks. We also perceive it to be the authoritative declaration of the meaning of covenant. The reader will notice that heretofore I have used the word *covenant* as a common noun. That usage will continue, but from here on, when I use the word to pertain to that arrangement between God and man, it will be capitalized to specify that it is not just any arrangement or contract but has to do with *the ultimate* of all arrangements, THE DIVINE COVENANT. If a Bible is lying nearby I want you to pick it up and hold it in your hand. It will be worth your while to find one and join me in this exercise.

The chances are you have not done before what I am suggesting you do now. Turn in your Bible to the title page. It will be either at the front or near, depending on how may helps your particular Bible has. It will read about like this:

THE
HOLY BIBLE
Containing the
OLD AND NEW TESTAMENTS

Ponder that scene for a few minutes. You are holding in your hand a Book that claims for itself the right to have the title **THE BOOK,** not merely a book. On virtually every continent in the world, when the term **THE BOOK** is used, someone in the company will know what is meant. But it is not just **THE BOOK** but THE **HOLY** BOOK, having God as its Supreme Author, Who, in His perfect providence, has decreed that what He desires to be said to us in written form is contained in this Book and separated as holy.

You and I need to ponder that often, and let it sink into the deep recesses of our thinking. The Bible not only contains the Word from God—IT IS THE WORD OF GOD! This statement, to me, in its totality, is so vital that, if we receive the first without the last part of it, we will be retreating from a posture that is absolute. If we do not have an absolute Word from God about Himself, we have no absolute place to begin to know God. His sovereignty declares and presupposes His ability to establish and maintain an absolute declaration about Himself.

Do you still have your Bible in hand? Don't lay it down. Below the designation on the title page of the Bible (THE HOLY BIBLE), you will find words identical or similar to these: CONTAINING THE OLD AND NEW TESTAMENTS. Now keep in mind, as I have already suggested, that the better translation for the word "Testament," at least in the light of modern word usage, is "Covenant." (We usually relegate the usage of "testament" to "will" as in "last will and testament." While there is this feature in the Scriptures, the Covenant of which I speak certainly covers more territory than a will as we use it in modern society!) Don't put your Bible down until you verbalize the following:

> I believe the Bible to be what it claims to be, THE WORD OF GOD. It is Holy in its Source because it came from God Himself. It is Holy in its content because it contains the mind of God. It is Holy in its intent because it has for its purpose salvation. It is divinely inspired, divinely preserved, and divinely illumined. I receive its truth, all of it as embraced in the Old and New Covenants. I accept it as accurate, final, and absolute truth as it pertains to God, man, the world, sin, salvation, and all else about which it speaks.

You may want to repeat and ponder key statements from the 1834 New Hampshire Confession of Faith regarding the Bible:

> It is a perfect treasure of divine instruction. It has God for its Author, salvation for its end, and truth, without any mixture of error, for its matter. It reveals the principles by which God judges us; and therefore is, and will remain to the end of the world the supreme standard by which all human conduct, creeds, and religious opinions should be tried.[1]

You may now lay your Bible down, but please keep it close to you.

The reason I have made much of the Bible at this point is: *Your knowledge of who you are is no more solid than the source from which it is derived. Our claim is that the Bible, and the Bible alone, makes clear our authentic identity. A solid sense of identity demands a solid sense of biblical authority!* This is precisely the reason for this little "side trip" back to biblical authority. In summary let me say that we have a clear Word on who we are within the pages of the Bible which is related to us within the framework of covenantal arrangements.

The History of Mankind on Earth

We not only have the Bible as a source but years of history after the canon of Bible to accentuate and support the truths it presents. It can be safely stated that of all the developments and discoveries in all areas of human knowledge, *not one* stands to discredit the Bible as a whole or any part of it in particular. Human history, then, has simply been one loud "Amen" to the credibility and reliability of the Bible. The Bible is right!

Let's look at history, particularly as it relates to the truths about covenants in general. There is serious question as to whether there exists on this earth a nation, tribe, cult, or collection of people where there are not features of covenant derived from the biblical idea of Blood Covenant. This would doubtlessly include even (if not especially) organized crime with its laws and symbols.

We find in these historical reflections not only support for the credibility of the covenant idea in general but some clarification of the Biblical Covenant, even in what one calls the "garbled" versions of human covenant. However "garbled" or degraded these more modern covenants are, or have been, they record something of the seriousness of the original from which they are all derived. And with this there comes the undeniable fact that I have repeated elsewhere: *the idea of covenant and identity are bound inseparably together!* Let's look at some of these "garbled" versions of covenant. These illustrations are taken from H. Clay Trumbull's book, *The Blood Covenant.*

The Flow of Blood Indicating Affection

At the beginning of the eighteenth century the French ambassador to Turkey noted in his journals certain Oriental manners. Among them was a Turkish lover gashing his arm in the presence of his lady-love, as a proof of his loving attachment to her. The accompanying statement with this act is that the relative flow of blood thus devoted indicated the measure of affection.[2]

A missionary to the South Sea islands wrote of an interesting custom relating to a blood covenant. A shark's tooth was used to draw blood to indicate gladness or grief and, in either event, it was apparent that the blood itself, not the suffering, was what counted as proof of love and devotion. A historian, writing about this, related an event which found his party sailing into an isthmus. When they came within a short distance of the shore an aged woman, who had worked for him, welcomed the party back by striking herself on the head with a shark's tooth until the blood flowed down to her shoulders. Those accompanying her watched in complete passivity.[3]

In one of Grimm's folk-lore fairy tales of the North there is the story of a queen's daughter going away from home, attended by a single servant. As the time of the daughter's departure arrived the mother took her daughter into a chamber and there, with a knife, cut her own finger with it, allowing the blood to drop on a napkin beneath. She allowed three drops of blood to fall on the napkin after which she handed it to the daughter, saying, "Dear child, preserve this well, and it will help you out of trouble." *That blood represented the mother's very life!* It was accustomed to speak out in words of counsel and warning to the daughter. But by and by the napkin was lost, and then the power of the young princess was gone, and the poor princess was alone in the wide world, at the mercy of strangers. How wonderful is this pagan illustration to convey such a divine truth. The blood of Jesus represents His very life.[4]

By that blood we overcome the evil one. We sing:

> The blood that Jesus shed for me,
> Way back on Calvary,
> The blood that gives me strength from day to day,
> Shall never lose its power.

"They overcame him (the Accuser) by the blood of the Lamb . . ." (Rev. 12:11*a*). What was being indicated here? *That the life of Jesus, represented in the blood, was the means of victory!*

By the way, does this not strike a strange resemblance to the Canaanitish worship of Baal on Mount Carmel when they became frantic and jumped upon the altar, crying aloud and cutting themselves until the blood gushed out?

Trumbull further observed, "Similar methods of showing love for God are in vogue today (1885 at Trumbull's writing) among the natives of Armenia. It is observed that one would cut his forehead with a sword and allow the blood to flow onto a sort of sheet that was worn in front. It was perceived, not as an act of self-torture, but as proof of self-devotedness, the very life of one being resident in the blood."[5]

The Blood and Commitment or Identification

A woman on trial, during the days of "witchfinding" in England in the seventeenth century, was reported as being highly dissatisfied with her trials where she was employed. One night when she was in bed she heard a knock at the door. Out the window she saw a tall black man and asked him his business. He replied that he was discontented about her trials and that he would put her into an arrangement where she would never lack for anything. She let him in, and he told her that first he must see her hand. Taking her hand he cut it in the palm so a little blood was shed. He then took out a little book and requested that she write her name in it. She refused, but he guided her hand to sign her name. When this was finished he asked her to tell him whatever she needed. In signing her name with her own blood, she had pledged her life to this tall black man who would, in turn, meet her every need.[6]

Cotton Mather, in his *Wonders of the Invisible World,* citing a Swedish trial for witchcraft in which the possessed children were witnesses, stated that the witches were compelled to give themselves to the devil and vow they would serve him. This ceremony was completed as they would cut their fingers and write their names in his book.[7]

While such a study of covenanting in human history is interesting, my sharing it with you has a far more important purpose, namely to bear upon your soul the indelible and unforgettable impression that your identity is a *Covenant matter!* Our identity with Jesus Christ is a matter of Blood Covenant. Blood-letting is life-giving; life-giving is love-showing; love-showing is heart-yearning. These ideas are true of pagan blood rites, and they were taken from the original version which was a type of the shedding of the blood of Jesus as "the blood of the everlasting covenant" (Heb. 13:20).

Uses of Pagan Covenants to Spread the Gospel

There have been cases in the history of missions endeavors in which unbridled freedom to share the Gospel was brought about by some form of covenant with heathen tribes. Along the Southwestern border of the Chinese Empire, in Burma, the rite of blood-friendship was practiced, at least until relatively recent days. The missionary historian, R. M. Luther, wrote that the blood-covenant was well-known and commonly practiced among the Karens of Burma. He that there were three common methods of initiating the covenant.

First, there was the common method of eating together and, while not binding, it suggested the cessation of hostilities with the coming together for prospective covenanting in mind.

Second, there was the planting of a sapling tree. This was generally accompanied by certain ceremonies in which the covenanting parties would pledge peace as long as the tree lived. This was still not finally binding but more serious than the first method of eating together.

Third, there is the blood-covenant. This always involved the shedding and mingling of blood by the tribal representatives. Blood was drawn from the thigh, as the strongest part of the body, and touched to the lips of the covenant representatives. In some cases the blood was actually drunk. The historian further comments, "This covenant is of utmost force. It covers not only peace and truce but the promise of mutual assistance in both peace and war. In the case of chiefs there is the embracing of the entire tribe of the other chief . . . I never heard of the blood-covenant being broken."

He further set forth that in a few isolated instances a missionary would enter into a covenant with one of the Karen tribes. In one such case the missionary found the agreement to cover not only himself but his continuing offspring, as well as anyone who would marry his offspring. This particular missionary was forced into a fifteen-year absence from his mission field. During that time he received repeated word from that Karen tribe, asking, "When will you come back to *your people?*"[8]

Such a blood-covenant gave a foreigner every right he would have had if he had been born a member of that tribe. In some regions of that country it was unsafe for a stranger to travel unless a blood-covenant was made with the tribal chiefs. If such were the case, travel was absolutely safe. When the covenant was "cut" total identity was made with those covenanting tribes, their influence and resources claimed, and their complete commitment received. Thus, again the matters of *identity and covenant* are seen bound together in the history of covenanting, a point I insist on keeping constantly before you.

The most famous of missionary-related blood-covenanting stories are those told by and about Livingstone and Stanley. The continent of Africa has known as much or more about the "covenant of strong friendship" as any part of the world.

Livingstone made such a covenant quite by accident while performing an operation on a woman. As he was removing a tumor from among the muscles of her forearm, one of the small arteries burst, landing a few drops of blood in Dr. Livingstone's eye. As he was wiping the blood from his eye the woman remarked, "You were a friend before; now you are a blood-relation; and when you are in this way always send me word, that I may cook for you."

In the case of Henry M. Stanley, the blood-covenant was often a means of powerful protection and relief in times of need. The most notable illustration of this had to do with Mirambo, a powerful chieftan, who was compared by Stanley in warfare leadership with Frederick the Great and Napoleon. In 1871 Stanley encountered the forces of Mirambo and was badly beaten. Stanley described this powerful chief as one "feared by native and foreigner from Usui to Urori, and from Uvinza to Ugogo, an area covering 90,000 square miles." Seeing that he could neither avoid his influence and power nor best him in battle, Stanley decided upon seeking a "covenant of strong friendship" with Mirambo. Contact was made, and the meeting of these heroes was arranged. A blood-covenant was initiated which brought not only peace but identification of resources and powers. They became friends and brothers in a sacred covenant—life for life. They ate together, exchanged gifts, and mingled their blood, voicing their unselfish faithfulness for the remainder of their lives.

All in all Stanley cut the covenant with at least fifty tribes in Africa. While many missionaries viewed the covenant as a heathen rite, Stanley found his recognition of it to be a key that opened the doors for the Gospel of Jesus Christ.

On another occasion Stanley's party was facing starvation in 1877. They were unable to purchase food or approach a settlement or tribe with any rapport at all. It was only through blood-covenant that they were spared as they entered into strong friendship with tribe after tribe. One of these was with Itsi, king of Ntamo. Itsi named Stanley's milk goat as his preferred covenant gift and, after some negotiation, the goat was transferred. Some sources indicate that Stanley found in the goat's milk a help for the healing of his stomach, which may explain the hesitation in the exchange. Nevertheless the covenant was completed and after the ceremony they parted. Four years later Stanley and his party were in the area and encountered Ngalyema of Ntamo. Upon seeing him, Stanley recognized him to be none other than Itsi with whom he had covenanted four years previously.

But he had changed! He was now proud, covetous, and grasping like other lawless barbarians. He was prone to be cruel and evil in his humor. He had become a pupil of superstition and a slave to fetishes. Stanley was in the region in interest of the International Association of the Congo, and the destiny of that association was in the hands of none other than Itsi or Ngalyema, as he was disposed to call himself.

The king recognized Stanley as his blood-brother but made harsh demands upon that covenant friendship. He requested she asses, a gold-embroidered coat, jewelry, a large mirror, long brass chains, and other expensive commodities. The only gift Stanley received in return from the king was his sceptre, which was a long staff, banded with brass and coiled with brass wire. It was worth nothing compared with what the king had taken in salable items, but as Stanley carried that staff it represented his alliance, yea his identity, with a most powerful African chieftan. When, in the midst of what seemed to be unfair negotiations, Stanley suggested that it might be better to cancel their brotherhood, "No, no, no," cried Ngalyema (Itsi); "our brotherhood cannot be broken; our blood is now one." Through that pact and relationship, peace and good-will were accomplished in the region.

History is filled with such stories as these which give credibility to the Covenant from which they all spring. It is unfortunate that in our Western culture there is little left of the spirit of Covenant as it is presented in the Bible and strangely preserved in some primitive form by heathen cultures. What an ironic turn of events that we should observe where technology has had its greatest strides forward, relationships among people have suffered the most, while in some remote heathen regions of the planet, peace is preserved and human relationships are intact because of *a working knowledge of the nature of covenant!*

I have occupied these pages to underline the fact that on the foundation of the Divine Covenant with man through the blood of Jesus Christ, we can build the structure of proper identification as Covenant People.

In Chapter 5 we will discuss that Covenant of Covenants, the New Covenant in Christ.

5

The Covenant of Covenants: A Sure Foundation

"And He took the cup and gave thanks, and gave it to them saying, 'Drink ye all of it; for this is my blood of the new testament (New Covenant), which is shed for many for the remission of sins' " (Matt. 26:27-28).

If the Church of Century Twenty could see the implications of that statement there would surely be a spiritual awakening that would cause all others in history to pale into insignificance. We come in this division to view the heart and soul of our identity as individuals and as corporate members of the Body of Christ, the New Covenant.

The Unity of Covenant

From man's point of view there have been several distinct covenants. We have observed these expressions in a previous chapter. I stated that, in my opinion, from God's point of view it seems that He sees one basic Covenant with several expressions in the Old Testament (or Covenant).

From the evidence of the Bible's divisions, the Old Testament and the New Testament, it appears that such an opinion is supported. If that is in question it is still safe to conclude that there was an Old Covenant, an impermanent and incomplete one, that gave way to a New Covenant which was indeed permanent and complete. Some believe that the term Old Testament refers specifically and solely to the Sinaitic or Mosaic Covenant. The chief reason for this opinion is that about 150 of the more than 280 references in the Old Testament to the Covenant refer to the Covenant of Law at Sinai. What you choose to believe about this specific point does not alter the paramount truth conveyed by the whole idea of the Covenant, *that it makes up the indestructible foundation for determining who we are!*

The Contrast of Covenants

Paul, in Galatians 4:24, made it clear that he was referring to the Covenant of Law when he wrote, ". . . for these are the two covenants, the one from Mount Sinai which gendereth bondage . . ."

The writer of Hebrews, "In that he saith, a New covenant he hath made the first old. Now that which decayeth and waxeth old is ready to vanish away" (8:13).

Before we launch into a discussion of the New Covenant I want us to view it in contrast to the Old Covenant. The key word here is "better," as evidenced in the comparison of the Old and New Covenants given in Hebrews 8:6:

> But now hath he obtained a more excellent ministry by how much also he is the mediator of a better covenant, which was established on better promises.

The Covenant of the Old Order was good, whether it was with reference to Adam, Noah, Abraham, Moses, or David—or all together. But the word is that the New Covenant is *better.* Let us an observe a visual comparison to see how *much better* the New Covenant is than the old one:

OLD COVENANT	NEW COVENANT
Came by sinful man	Came by the sinless Christ
Temporary	Permanent
Incomplete	Complete
Conditional	Unconditional
Graven in stones	Written in the heart

External manifestation	Internal appropriation
Obedience demanded	Obedience enabled
Failed in man's disobedience	Succeeds in His obedience
The heart of man was wrong.	The heart of man is changed.
Of the letter which kills	Of the Spirit Who gives life
Makes me say "I ought"	I can say, "In Him, I can."
Provisional and preparatory	Ultimate and sufficient
Condemnation and death	Righteousness and life
Of passing glory	Of permanent glory
There was covering provided.	There was cleansing provided.
Gave demands but no power	Gives power by His Spirit
Was closed by the death of Christ	Was initiated by His death and resurrection
For Israel	For Israel and all the saved

A Legal Document Signed in the Court of Heaven

> Behold, the days come, saith the Lord, that I will make a new covenant with the house of Israel, and with the house of Judah: Not according to the covenant that I made with their fathers in the day I took them by the hand to bring them out of the land of Egypt; which my covenant they brake, although I was an husband unto them, saith the Lord:
>
> But this shall be the covenant that I will make with the house of Israel; After those days, saith the Lord, I will put my law in their inward parts, and write it in their hearts; and will be their God, and they shall be my people.
>
> And they shall teach no more every man his neighbour, saying, Know the Lord: for they shall all know me, from the least of them to the greatest of them, saith the Lord: for I will forgive their iniquity, and I will remember their sin no more" (Jer. 31:31-34).

And this document, decreed in heaven, is the heart of the Gospel. Surely with that knowledge in mind Paul affirmed,

"For I am not ashamed of the gospel of Christ: for it is the power of God unto salvation to everyone that believeth; to the Jew first, and also to the Greek. For therein is the righteousness of God revealed from faith to faith: as it is written, the just shall live by faith (Rom. 1:16-17)."

The essential terms of that New Covenant are repeated in Hebrews 8:8-12. Let us stay here long enough to assess the qualities of this New Covenant, with the knowledge that this is the "spiritual stuff on which our essential identity is constructed."

In Sin a Hopeless Identity

Outside of Divine Covenant you and I have no valid identities. In sin we are quite another species than God made us to be. We are born into sin with every part of our beings touched and tainted by sin. We will discuss this as we come to view the old man and the new man in a later chapter.

But how can a basic identity be changed when there are wrong desires, motives, and no inner spiritual equipment for fellowship with a Holy God? It is a hopeless situation on mankind's side. Anything that is done must be done on God's part, and that is exactly what the New Covenant is about.

A New Law and a New Heart

In the Old Order the presence of God was an outward manifestation—a pillar of fire, a glory cloud. But under God's new covenant His Life has a new dwelling place, the regenerated, reconstructed human heart. God promised, "I will put my law in their inward parts, and write it in their hearts." This Covenant promise can only be fulfilled in the new birth. God's laws can only be put into regenerated minds. God has engaged in the Covenant to work in us.

A new heart also will I give you, and a new spirit will I put within you: and I will take away your stony heart out of your flesh, and I will give you a heart of flesh. And I will pour out my Spirit within you, and cause you to walk in my statutes, and ye shall keep my judgments and do them (Ezek. 36:27).

A New Standing with God

God has promised to be "their God." In Covenant He is with us and allows us to refer to Him as *our* God. But that is only one side of it. He is glad to own us as *His* people. Now the temple of the Living God is man himself. We are a Spirit-people, indwelt by the Holy Spirit and marked as God's own people. This New Covenant has no power to save except through the presence of the Holy Spirit. He is the Great Gift of the Covenant. He is the Teacher of what the Covenant means. He is the Revealer of Jesus Christ, the Mediator of the New Covenant.

THE NEW COVENANT A RESULT OF COVENANT IN ETERNITY PAST

Spurgeon imagines the Covenant Council of Eternity and gives the Trinity these words: "I, the Most High Jehovah, do hereby give unto My only begotten and well-loved Son, a people, countless beyond the number of the stars, who shall by Him be washed from sin, by Him preserved and kept, and led, and by Him, at last, presented before My throne, without spot or wrinkle, or any such thing. I covenant by oath and swear by Myself, because I can swear by no greater, that these whom I now give to Christ shall be forever the objects of My eternal love. Them will I forgive through the merit of the blood. To these I give a perfect righteousness; these will I adopt and make My sons and daughters, and they shall reign with Me through Christ eternally.

"The Holy Spirit also, as one of the contracting parties on this side of the Covenant, gave this declaration, 'I hereby covenant that all whom the Father giveth to the Son, I will in due time quicken. I will show them their need of redemption; I will cut off from them all groundless hope, and destroy their refuge of lies. I will bring them to the blood of sprinkling; I will give them faith whereby this blood shall be applied to them; I will work in them every grace; I will keep their faith alive; I will cleanse them and drive out all depravity from them, and they shall be presented at last spotless and faultless.'

"The Lord Jesus Christ, before time began, covenanted with the Father and with the Spirit, 'On my part of the Covenant I in due time will become a man. I will take upon Myself the form and nature of fallen man. I will live in their wretched world, and for My people I will keep the Law perfectly. I will work out a spotless righteousness, which shall be acceptable to the demands of God's just and holy Law. In due time I will bear the sins of My people. God will exact their debts on Me; the chastisement of their peace will I endure, and by My stripes they shall be healed. I covenant and promise that I will be obedient unto death, even the death of the cross. I will magnify Thy law and make it honorable. I will suffer all that they ought to have suffered. I will endure the curse of Thy law, and all the vials of Thy wrath shall be emptied and spent upon My head. I will rise again; I will ascend into heaven; I will intercede for them at Thy right hand; and I will make Myself responsible for every one of them, that not one of those whom thou hast given Me shall ever be lost, but I will bring all My sheep of whom, by the blood, Thou hast constituted me the Shepherd . . . I will bring every one safe to thee at last.' "[1]

And so ran the Covenant before time began. Thus, before we arrived on earth our identities were sealed as a Covenant people, sealed with the blood of the Everlasting Covenant. That Eternal Covenant, so agreed upon in eternity past, is our *sure foundation.*

6
Meet the Mediator: The Christ of the Covenant

Back of all the covenants and before all the covenants which God made with men stands a Covenant which God made with His Own Son in the councils of eternity. All covenantal expressions issue from this Covenant. Who He, The Christ, is and what He has done form the *Legal Document* which certifies our true identity.

A basic understanding of salvation awaits a basic understanding of the character and work of Christ as He relates to the New Covenant. In the previous chapter we read Spurgeon's wonderful depiction of that Eternal Agreement within the Trinity. It is vital to remember that the whole of the salvation drama was prompted, not by man's rebellion as if it were unexpected, but by the very decrees of God the Father, God the Spirit, and God the Son. Thus, long before election, long before creation, long before there was sin, and long before there was anything, *there was the Eternal Mediator, Jesus Christ.*

We will view in this chapter five designations of the work of Christ as to the Covenant. As you meditate on them do not forget that these form the bases for truth about everything which touches upon who you are.

Christ the Mediator

> In the beginning was the Word, and the Word was with God, and the Word was God. The same was in the beginning with

> God; all things were made by him and without him was not anything made that was made (John 1:1-3).

This Mediatorship was not a suddenly-contrived affair. Jesus was the Lamb slain *from the foundation of the world* (see Rev. 13:8). Paul called it "a secret kept since the world began" (Rom. 16:25).

Three times in Hebrews, Jesus is referred to as the Mediator of the New Covenant:

> But now hath he obtained a more excellent ministry, by how much also he is the mediator of a better covenant, which was established upon better promises (8:6).
>
> And for this cause he is the mediator of the new Testament, that by means of death, for the redemption of the transgressions that were under the first testament, that they which are called might receive the promise of the eternal inheritance (9:15).
>
> And to Jesus the mediator of the new covenant, and to the blood of sprinkling, that speaketh better things than that of Abel (12:24).

The word for "mediator" in the Greek is *mesites* made up of two words, one meaning "middle" and the other meaning "to go." Thus the meaning of this most important word is "to go between." A mediator, then, is one who goes between two parties with a view toward producing peace. However, the mediation of Christ involves more than this. Our salvation requires that the Mediator should Himself possess the nature and attributes of Him towards whom He acts, and should likewise participate in the nature of those for whom He acts; only by being both of Deity and humanity should He comprehend the claims of one and the needs of the other.[1]

Paul declared to Timothy, "For there is one God and one mediator between God and men, the man Christ Jesus" (1 Tim. 2:5). *That mediation, it must be remembered, is from eternity to eternity.* It was being carried on a million years ago in your behalf and mine. It will be going on a million years from now.

It is going on at this moment. It will never cease. His mediation is eternal. We are saved forever because His is a *hands-on* redemption.

Christ the Surety

> By so much was Jesus made a surety of a better testament (Heb. 7:22).

While there are overlapping facets in the matters of mediation and surety, they are far from identical. The Greek word for "surety" is *enguos* which, Vines says, primarily signifies bail, the bail which answers for everyone whether with life or property.[2]

The scripture prior to Hebrews 7:22 answers the question as to the connection of Jesus with the Covenant. "The Lord sware and will not repent [change], Thou art a high priest for ever after the order of Melchisedec." Thus, it is clear that this suretyship is established by and anchored to God's oath, so stated in Hebrews 7:21*b*.

A surety, when it is designated as a person, is one who stands good for another. In the case of Christ, He stands good for all Covenant parties. *He stands surety with us for God,* that God's part in the Covenant will be faithfully performed. *He stands surety with God for us,* that our part in the Covenant will be faithfully performed. How glorious! He makes God's faithfulness and ours equally secure.

Another legal word synonomous with surety is *guarantee.* Jesus Christ, in His Person, is the Eternal Guarantor of this New Covenant. Add to that His office as Eternal Mediator, and you have an eternally-sealed covenant.

By the time we are through we will have viewed His work of surety in eternity past, on the cross, and on the throne. But His work continues past that. He continues His work of surety in our hearts. And here in our hearts the genius of the New Covenant takes place. Here the New Covenant has its glorious triumph. He legally establishes our authentic *identity* in the Covenant, and He enables the appropriation of Covenant privileges and power. Andrew Murray put it well, "No surety was ever so faithful to his undertaking as Jesus will be to His on our behalf in our hearts."[3] But even this is not all He is!

Christ the High Priest

He has been declared by God's oath "as a priest for ever after the order of Melchisedek" (Heb. 7:21*b*). His priesthood and His suretyship are bound together in the same oath. When God gives an oath about anything, it means that the matter about which He had made the oath is unconditionally guaranteed. In this case it is the eternality of Jesus' priesthood and suretyship. There are several words connected with this priesthood which are meaningful to us:

It is an *unchangeable* priesthood (Heb. 7:24).

It is a priesthood which *enables uttermost salvation* (Heb. 7:25*a*).

It is a priesthood *of eternally continuous intercession* (Heb. 7:25*b*).

It is a priesthood that is *holy, harmless, undefiled, separate from sinners, and made higher than the heavens* (Heb. 7:26).

It is a priesthood brought about not by law of men but by *an oath of God* (Heb. 7:28).

It is a priesthood of One *set on the right hand of the throne of the Majesty in the heavens* (Heb. 8:1). (Ground for our claiming to be "a royal priesthood"—1 Pet. 2:9)

Now we have an Eternal Mediator, an Eternal Surety, and an Eternal Priest operating an Eternal Covenant. But even this is not all!

Christ Our Sacrifice

For such an high priest became us, who is holy, harmless,

> undefiled, separate from sinners, and made higher than the heavens.
>
> Who needeth not daily, as those high priests, to offer up sacrifice, first for his own sins, and then for the people's; for this He did once, when He offered up Himself (Heb. 7:26-27)."

Imagine it, the Mediator, the Surety, the Priest . . . is also the *sacrifice!* The one sacrifice that Jesus made, Himself, ended the slaughtering of animals and the carrying of blood into the Holy of Holies. He, as the Mediator, *initiated* the Covenant in eternity past and now remains the *expiation* or sacrifice which continues to satisfy God's violated holiness.

And what is the result of this sacrifice? Listen to the answer in Hebrews 10:12-14:

> But this man [Christ], after he had offered one sacrifice for sins for ever, sat down at the right hand of God;
>
> From henceforth expecting til his enemies be made his footstool.
>
> For by one offering he hath perfected for ever them that are sanctified.

He is recognized as our *Advocate,* our attorney. *Webster's Dictionary* says that an advocate is one "who pleads the cause of another in a court of law; one who defends, vindicates, or espouses a cause by argument; an upholder, a defender, one summoned to aid." Our Attorney is activated when we confess our sins. Can the outcome of our confession be in doubt when the Attorney we have called is the Mediator, the Surety, the High Priest, and the Sacrifice of the New Covenant? But there is more that—He is:

Christ the Author and Finisher of Our Faith

The difficulty in establishing and maintaining our proper sense of identity lies in the direction of our attention. Much of the time we are watching and listening to the world system, with our own minds influenced by the world, or, God forbid, to the accuser or his emissaries instead of "looking unto Jesus." The result is that we have a distorted or crippled sense of identity.

Here is our hope: "Looking unto Jesus the author and finisher of our faith; Who for the joy that was set before him endured the cross, despising the shame, and is set down at the right hand of the throne of God" (Heb. 12:2).

A constant concentration on Jesus as Author and Finisher of our faith will mean that all of His eternal work in behalf of the Covenant will be ours in daily living. As Author He chose to endure the cross, despising the shame; as Finisher He sits at the right hand of the throne of God to see through what He began. Just as He is the Author and Finisher of our faith, He is the Author and Finisher of our identity!

THE FOUNDATION OF OUR IDENTITY IS SECURE

E. W. Kenyon, in his poem, expressed it ably:

THE BLOOD COVENANT

I've a right to grace in the hardest place,
 On the ground of the Blood Covenant;
I've a right to peace that can never cease,
 On the ground of the Blood Covenant;
I've a right to joy that can never cloy,
 On the ground of the Blood Covenant;
I've a right to power, yes, this very hour,
 On the ground of the Blood Covenant;
I've a right to health, through my Father's wealth
 On the ground of the Blood Covenant;
I my healing take, Satan's hold must break,
 On the ground of the Blood Covenant.
I've a legal right, now to win this fight,
 On the ground of the Blood Covenant;
I will take my part with courageous heart
 On the ground of the Blood Covenant.
Now my rights I claim, in His Mighty Name,
 On the ground of the Blood Covenant;

And my prayers prevail, though all hell assail,
On the ground of the Blood Covenant.
On the ground of the Blood,
On the ground of the Blood Covenant;
I will claim my rights, though the enemy fights,
On the ground of the Blood Covenant.[4]

This glorious Blood Covenant—presided over by Christ, the Eternal Surety; vitally continued in the unceasing intercessions of Christ, our Eternal High Priest; forever validated by Christ, the Eternal Sacrifice—enables us to stand before God, the world, and the devil himself without guilt, feelings of inadequacy, shame, or fear. "Looking unto Jesus, the author and the finisher of our faith." For it was He, on the cross, Who not only removed the curses of a broken covenant, that the sinner might be pardoned; He met the demands of the Covenant in His life so a perfect keeping of the commandments (righteousness) might be imputed to every believer.

This leaves nothing for us to do but to consciously recognize our place *in Christ* and thus, *in covenant,* as the grounds of our essential identity, and proceed therefrom to a life of *Covenant living.*

My prayer for you as we end this section and prepare to begin another is found in Hebrews 13:20-21:

> Now the God of peace, who brought again from the dead our Lord Jesus, that great shepherd of the sheep, through the blood of the everlasting covenant, make you perfect in every good work, working in you that which is well-pleasing in his sight, through Jesus Christ; to whom be glory for ever and ever. Amen.

7
In Christ: The Position of Essential Identity

> Created *in Christ Jesus* unto good works (Eph. 2:10).
>
> Of him are ye *in Christ Jesus* . . . (1 Cor. 1:30).
>
> According as he hath chosen us *in him* before the foundation of the world (Eph. 1:4).
>
> And we are *in him* that is true, even in His Son Jesus Christ (1 John 5:20).

W. H. Griffith Thomas, in his book *Christianity Is Christ,* says, "Christianity is the only religion in the world which rests on the person of its founder."[1] I would go yet another step to state that only in Christianity is it true that the adherents find their authentic identities in the person of the Founder.

About twenty years after my salvation experience I discovered what I now call *the Gospel for the saved.* Unfortunately, when I was saved there was no one around who seemed eager to explain what had happened to me. I supposed that everyone thought I would find out somewhere somehow. I was called to preach and quickly committed my life to the ministry, but it required about twenty years for me to discover: Just as the Gospel is "good news" to the lost, it is also "good news" to the saved. The good news is that the same Jesus, who in His death had paid the penalty for the guilt of my sin, was very much alive in me in the Person of the Holy Spirit to validate in and through me what had been done for me on the Cross. My first book, *The*

Key to Triumphant Living, is the testimony of this blessed discovery and its attendant blessings.

And yet, as glorious and life-altering as the discovery of that truth—Christ in me—was, I soon discovered it was only half of the blessed truth that lies at the heart of my relationship with God. That truth is simply *our union with Christ.* Yes, Christ *is* in me, but, praise the Lord, I *am* in Him. Those blessed facts are two sides of the coin of salvation—He is in me and I am in Him.

> Ian Thomas expresses it eloquently: To be *in Christ* . . . this is redemption; but for Christ to be *in you* . . . that is sanctification; to be *in Christ* . . . that makes you fit for heaven; but for Christ to be *in you* . . . that makes you fit for earth! To be *in Christ* that changes your destination; but for Christ to be *in you* .. that changes your destiny! The one makes heaven your home, the other makes this world His workship![2]

With this truth, our union with Christ, I want to deal briefly in this chapter. But to do so I first want us to take a backward step by viewing it . . .

IN CONTRAST TO WHO WE WERE *IN ADAM*

We can best understand our new identity in Christ by facing our old identity in Adam. When we were born into this world we were born into a kingdom, a family, and a race. We had nothing to do with it, no choice in the matter. It was merely a matter of birth. In like manner when you and I were born we were born into the larger family of Adam. Adam, ancestor to us all, acted as our representative when he chose to sin, resulting in the fall. Before you yell "Unfair!" you should hear the whole story. (Jesus Christ acted as our representative as well when He died on the cross for our sins!)

There is a sense, then, in which we were all "born dead"! We were born into Adam's race, in Adam, as it were and thus in sin, which is death. We have a clear description of who we were in Adam in Ephesians 2. I will list the qualities of the *in Adam* existence and briefly comment on each of them:

Dead in Trespasses and Sin (Eph. 2:1)

Outside of Christ we were alive in our bodies but dead to God in the realm of the spirit. We had biological life but no spiritual life. We were not simply dead—we were dead in sin. Being in Adam, though, we were not responsible for his sin; we were, when born, ruined by his sin.

We Walked According to the Course of This World (Eph. 2:2a)

Because we were of Adam's family we were born rebels which guaranteed that we would walk in accordance with a fallen world system. Our sin was systemic: that is, it was not simply a matter of wrong acting—it was a matter of wrong being. The whole system was pervaded with sin. This is the reason we cannot hope to legislate righteousness in a society of unredeemed people. They will act out the nature that is within them, Adam's!

We Were Indwelt with a Spirit of Disobedience (Eph. 2:2b)

We have the continuing description of the profound human problem in the following verse:

> Among whom also we all had our conversation [conduct] in times past in the lusts of the flesh, fulfilling the desires of the flesh and of the mind; and were by nature the children of wrath, even as others (Eph. 2:3).

We were influenced by a spirit but not the Holy Spirit. We produced unholy actions because we were influenced by an unholy spirit. We just acted out our authentic identity as sinners.

We Were Without Christ and Aliens from the Commonwealth of Israel (Eph. 2:12a)

We were *without* and *outside* Christ. That plainly agrees with 1 John 5:12, "He that hath the Son hath life; and he that hath not the Son of God hath not life." Being outside of Christ put us out of the family of God, "the commonwealth of Israel" Commonwealth means "politics"—we were outside the political affiliation of Israel as a people of God.

Strangers to the Covenants of Promise (Ephesians 2:12b)

We were not included in the promises of the covenants in our unregenerate state. We were thus "without hope and without God in the world." Let's then summarize our identity as we were in Adam.

Dead
Rebellious
Indwelt of evil spirit
Without Christ
Aliens to God's family
Strangers to covenants
Without hope
Without God

BUT NOW—*IN CHRIST*

I was born into the Taylor family because my biological father was a Taylor. It was determined even before I was born. At the same time I was born biologically as a Taylor I was born spiritually as an *Adamite,* after the father of us all. But one glad day I was born again, this time into the Christ family. I received the Christ nature. The word used to describe my relationship with Christ more than 150 times is the little word "*in.*" I am now *in* Christ. As I found my inevitable identity as an unregenerate man in Adam, I now find my identity in Christ. As surely as I was identified correctly as a Taylor at my birth, I am now identified as a Christ-one, a Christian, at my new birth. *In Christ* is my essential identity. What does it mean to be in Christ? Let us observe:

Alive
Righteous
Indwelt by Holy Spirit
In Christ
One with Christ
In Covenant
In union
Redeemed
Sanctified
Glorified
Overcomer

TO BE IN CHRIST IS TO BE IN COVENANT

In Christ, God and man have become one in a covenant union which can never be dissolved. To be in Christ is to be in

Israel. The covenant promises belong to every believer in Jesus. In Ephesians 2:12 we read,

> That at that time ye were without Christ, being aliens from the commonwealth of Israel, and strangers from the covenants of promise . . ."

Then in the next verse, Ephesians 2:13, we read,

> But now *in Christ Jesus* ye who were sometimes afar off are made nigh by the blood of Christ."

We were separated; now we are joined with Jesus. Our new sphere is Christ. I want you to envision the circle in the illustration as a three-dimensional circle or a sphere. The flat circle does not tell it all. We are in the sphere of Christ. We are joined to Him as inside Him. He is inside us. This is union at its most intimate. The word *in* is best understood in terms of Covenant. I am spiritually joined to Him. "He that is joined to the Lord is one spirit" (1 Cor. 6:17).

I never again have the right to speak of myself as separate from Christ or to listen to lies about being separated from Him. As in the blood-covenants of old, in the New Covenant I have all that He has, and He has all that I have! He has become one with me and I, one with Him! S. D. Gordon, in his book succintly entitled *In Christ*

> If one is in Christ, he must have *regeneration;* for how can the Head be alive and the members be dead?
>
> If one is in Christ, he must be *justified;* for how can God condemn the Head and condemn the members?
>
> If one is in Christ, he must have *sanctification;* for how can the spotlessly holy remain in vital connection with that which is unholy?
>
> If one is in Christ, he must have *redemption;* for how can the Son of God be in glory, while that which He has made a part of His Body lies abandoned in the grave of eternal death?[3]

TO BE IN CHRIST IS TO BE IN CHRIST ETERNALLY

I have never tried to explain this in print before this moment. I want you to read this slowly and again if necessary. I will attempt to arrange the words where you can see their importance with the greatest of possible ease and then understand their meaning.

There was a time when I was in Adam . . .
I was in Adam's past and Adam's future,
Adam's past was my past; Adam's future was mine.
All the condemnation that accrued to Adam's sin was mine . . .
All the weakness of the Adamic nature was mine . . .
BUT THEN ONE DAY . . .
My life in Adam was terminated . . .
I WAS PLACED INTO CHRIST!
Now I am in Christ, completely and eternally . . .
I am in Christ's future, Christ's present,
AND I AM IN CHRIST'S PAST.
Though there was an historical time, before I was regenerated, when I was in Adam . . .
Once in Christ, it is as if I had no history in Adam at all . . . no record of my past.
Now, in Christ, I have always been there.
For the record, God's record, when you review my record, you will find only Christ in my past!
What I am now, in my essential identity in Christ, I have always been in God's eyes, in His record.
For, you see, *I was chosen in Him before the foundation of the world, that I should be holy and without blame before Him in love; having been predestinated unto the adoption of children by Jesus Christ to Himself, according to the good pleasure of His will* (See Eph. 1:4-5).

Do you understand what you have just read? Read it again! Now, do you understand it? Of course not! It is beyond human understanding. It is a mystery of mysteries in which we will revel in eternity. You ask, "How could a believer be in Christ when he did not yet exist." I ask you another question, not to confuse, but to demonstrate the fact that there is no explainable answer, "How could God elect and love a soul which He had not yet created?" The answer to both questions is: *"I don't know how, but I know that he (the believer) was and that He (God) did!"*

TO BE IN CHRIST IS TO BE IN ALL THAT HE DID AND IS

F. J. Huegel in his classic *Bone of His Bone* wrote "The Christian life is a participation . . . not an imitation."[4] We are commanded to be holy as He is holy, to love our enemies, to pray for those who despitefully use us, to be careful (anxious) for nothing, to give thanks always, and etc., etc., ad infinitum, ad nauseum. Impossible? Yes! But we have been informed that we have become one in spirit with Christ (1 Cor. 6:17); that we have become partakers of the Divine nature (1 Pet. 1:4); that we are made partakers of Christ (Heb. 3:14); that we are the branches and He the vine (John 15:1). The commands to us in the Bible are impossible to an *imitator* but not to a *participant!*

We are one with Christ in his *crucifixion*—His death is ours. We have a right to, "I am crucified with Christ; nevertheless I live; yet not I, but Christ liveth in me, and the life which I now live in the flesh, I live by the faith of the Son of God, who loved me and gave himself for me (Gal. 2:20)." His death, now ours, is legal payment for our sin. We are justified, as justified as if we had never sinned or (just as significantly) just as if we had died for our own sin!

We are one with Christ in His *resurrection;* His glorious resurrection life is ours. Not only did you and I die with Christ, in Him we arose. Death was but the transition to resurrection life and abundance. We possess in our bodies, we who are redeemed, the resurrection life of Jesus Christ. We are one with that life!

We are one with Christ in His *ascension;* his ascension is ours. We not only have been raised from the dead, but we have been elevated to sit with Him in the heavenlies: "And hath raised us up together, and made us to sit together in heavenly places *in Christ Jesus* (Eph. 2:6)."

We are one with Christ in His *overcoming;* His victory is ours. Jesus Christ, as man in Whom dwelt the Spirit of God, conquered the devil, that mankind, indwelt by the Spirit of God, might maintain that already-won victory. We are overcomers, not because we have overcome, but because we are one with the Overcomer.

We are one with Him in his *glorification*; His glorification is ours. We have been informed of this in no uncertain terms:

> For whom he did *foreknow,* he also did *predestinate* to be conformed to the image of his Son, that he might be the firstborn among many brethren. Moreover whom he did predestinate, them he also called: and whom he called, them he also justified: and whom he justified, them he also *glorified* (Rom. 8:29-30).

All the words which refer to what happens to all "whoms" are in the past tense, which means, as a matter of God's record, they are completed. No wonder the next verse says, "What shall we then say to these things? If God be for us, who can be against us?"

I repeat it: we are one with all He did and is! First John 4:17 is a remarkable scripture which can be taken no other way than literally: "Herein is our love made perfect, that we may have boldness in the day of judgment: because *as He is so are we in this world.*"

I close this chapter with a challenge to you, my reader, to ponder these nine words which summarize our union with Christ:

AS HE IS
SO ARE WE
IN THIS WORLD!

Can you fathom that? No, but you can believe it by faith, because it is precisely what the Bible teaches. I challenge you to stop here before going on and repeat the following a dozen times or so:

AS HE IS
SO AM I
IN THIS WORLD!

8
A Prayer You Cannot Live Without

Wherefore I also, after I heard of your faith in the Lord Jesus, and love unto all the saints, cease not to give thanks for you, making mention of you in my prayers; that the God of our Lord Jesus Christ, the Father of glory, may give unto you the spirit of wisdom and revelation in the knowledge of him: That the eyes of your understanding being enlightened; that ye may know *what is the hope of his calling, and what the riches of the glory of his inheritance in the saints, and what is the exceeding greatness of his power to usward who believe, according to the working of his mighty power* (Eph. 1:15-19).

Prayer is a timeless miracle. It leaps beyond the borders of time and space and releases the power and life of God. The timelessness of prayer is especially appealing in its intrigue.

You and I can pray prayers today that can be effectual for yet unborn generations. We ourselves are benefactors of prayers that were prayed before we were born. Intercessions are circling our heads at this moment on the part of people whose lips have long since been muted by death, but God has not forgotten them.

Prayers prayed by the prophets of the Old Testament and by the apostles of the New Testament are still valid in our lives. The saints of the ages, their love, influence, and prayers, are a part of our heritage as God's new creations.

The prayer of Paul for the saints in Ephesus (1:15-19) is for you and me as well. God has been faithfully and wonderfully answering that prayer down through the ages of the Church. He wants to answer it for every saint, including you and me, now in this generation. I want to examine the prayer in general before we look at the specific requests.

That We May Have a Spirit of Wisdom and Revelation in the Knowledge of Him

In the general part of this prayer there are three important and powerful words: Wisdom, Revelation, and Knowledge. Paul has prayed that we have all three. They are ours to receive. They are a part of our inheritance. Let's look at these three words:

WISDOM: The word here is *sophia* and in references such as this always means a knowledge in relation to the regulation of the relationship with God. This kind of wisdom is described in James 3:17, "But the wisdom that is from above is first pure, then peaceable, gentle, and easy to be entreated, full of mercy and good fruits, without partiality, and without hyprcrisy." What a gift!

REVELATION: This is the same word used for the Book of Revelation. The word is *apocalupsis* which literally means "an unveiling or uncovering." It implies the removing of a veil of mystery. The Book of Revelation is an "unveiling" of the Lord Jesus Christ. Vines further clarifies it, as it appears here in Ephesians 1, as "a communication of the knowledge of God to the soul"[1]

KNOWLEDGE: This is a special word and is worthy of particular note. The Greek word is *epignosis* and means "a full perception or recognition." It carries the impact of participation. "Ye shall know the truth, and the truth shall make you free" (John 8:32). This is beyond what we perceive to be "knowing." It is participation, i.e., *epignosis,* that sets us free, not just an acquaintance with the thought processes. The fact that this knowledge is "of Him" makes it richer still. We are to participate in Him.

That the Eyes of Your Understanding Being Enlightened . . .

The literal translation of this is "that the eyes of your heart may be totally and continuously enlightened." The root word is *photidzo* from *phos* meaning "light." Paul is praying here that we may have a continuous experience of enlightenment. This word is in the perfect tense which always suggests continuous process.

That Ye May Know . . .

All of this is that we may *know something.* How important that *something* must be. The Holy Spirit has inspired and orchestrated this prayer for the church in all ages. It must have a high priority in heaven at this moment. The word here for "know" is yet another word. It is from the word *oida* which is from the root word meaning "to see." We often remark, when something is being explained, "Oh, I see!" This is what we call "an eye-opening experience." And that is what you are going to have in this chapter if you will allow the Holy Spirit to answer Paul's prayer. (This is what I have prayed for the reader as I have written it.)

I Proclaim a Parenthesis .

Change gears at this point and think with me about three of the greatest needs in the lives of human beings. I have yet to prove it, but I feel that these needs embrace within their reach all other needs experienced on earth. They are *security, significance,* and *sufficiency.* Every human being on earth seeks a sense of security, a sense of significance, and a sense of sufficiency. Our frustrations, heartaches, and needless tensions can be categorized under one of these prevalent needs. These are legitimate needs that every human will in time experience. Drives develop around these needs; the drive to *protect,* the drive to *perform,* and the drive to *produce.* These and other drives go into operation to seek the fulfilment of these needs. If they are not met legitimately, all sorts of problems develop. Human beings are feverishly searching for the satisfaction of these needs.

This little side trip into your legitimate needs will show you how perfectly practical Paul's prayer is for you. We will observe these matters according to need, problem, and solution.

NEED: A sense of security.

PROBLEM: Fear of harm and results therefrom

SOLUTION: Paul's number-one request—"That ye may know what is the hope of his calling" (Eph. 1:18*b*). This tends to be somewhat obscure in its statement. Let me see if I can help make the meaning more obvious.

I believe Paul, in essence, is saying, "Wake up to the fact that you have it made!" The word "hope" in the Bible always means "a certainty that needs no visible foundation on which to rest." You might write the word "certainty" over every word "hope" in your Bible and understand it better. We comprehend the word about faith a little better in this light: "Now faith is the substance of things hoped for [things we are certain of], the evidence of things not seen" (Heb. 11:1)." Our English word "hope" may vary in its meaning from wishful thinking to certainty. The New Testament word for "hope" always means certainty. The coming of Christ is called the blessed hope, not the blessed wish!

Of what does Paul want us to be certain? Of *His (God's) calling.* In other words, God can finish what He started. He can consummate what He commenced. I am secure in Him. My salvation rests, not on my ability to protect and preserve it, but upon His mighty power.

> The work which His goodness began,
> The arm of his strength will complete
> His promise is yea, and amen
> And never was forfeited yet.

Things future, nor things that are now,
Not all things below or above,
Can make Him His purpose forego,
Or sever my soul from His love.

My name from the palm of His hand,
Eternity will not erase,
Impressed on His heart it remains
In marks of indelible grace.
Yes, to the end I shall endure;
As sure as the earnest is given,
More happy but not more secure,
The glorified spirits in heaven.

Who needs protection beyond this? This is security as only God can provide it. Will you, at this moment, receive in vocal terms the answer to Paul's prayer in your life? Say aloud, "Father, I now receive the knowledge of the certainty of Your calling by faith!" Let's move to the next need.

NEED: A sense of *significance.*

PROBLEM: Fear of being a worthless nobody and resulting feelings and activities surrounding inferiority, hopelessness, and rejection.

SOLUTION: Paul's number-two request—"That ye may know . . . what the riches of the glory of his inheritance in the saints (Eph. 1:18*c*)." What an eye-opener! This is not pertaining to our inheritance as great as it is. This statement is in reference to *God's inheritance.* Did you know that God has an inheritance? And did you suppose that His inheritance was the galaxies, the solar systems, or the riches of the resources of the planets? This passage declares that *the riches of the glory of His inheritance is . . . in the saints!* We, you and I who are saved, make up His treasured inheritance. Paul has prayed that we might see how great are His riches because we are His own. Can we really believe that God so treasures us? Are we actually that important to Him? Is this part of what His love means to us? Yea and amen!

Feelings of insignificance and the resulting hopelessness have pressed upon all of us. We have been taught in the main that our net worth depends on the rightness of our performance. Sin has ravaged our self-consciousness, and we are left without identity, or at least a satisfying identity.

But here we see that the God who sits as Sovereign in this universe, Who owns everything and rules with the arm of His mighty power forever . . . counts us, as redeemed human beings, *His very own inheritance.*

Striving for significance can terminate. Seeking to win approval by performance can cease. Fears of rejection can be dismissed as groundless. Intimidating feelings of insignificance can be discarded once and for all. Our significance was both established and reflected at Calvary and is maintained with God Himself, as we remain in Covenant with Him through Jesus Christ. Hallelujah!

As long as you and I are made aware of this fact, we can never feel insignificant for long! But that is not all. Let's look at the next one.

NEED: A sense of *sufficiency.*

PROBLEM: Fear of helplessness, inadequacy, and inferiority resulting in damaging types of compensation.

SOLUTION: Paul's number-three request—"That ye may know . . . *what is the exceeding greatness of His power to us-ward who believe, according to the working of His* mighty power" (Eph. 1:19).

If the other two revelations are mighty and mysterious, this one excels in magnificence. Paul obviously felt a need to articulate this facet of his prayer more fully and illustrate it thoroughly. So he took off in all grammatical directions at once in a sentence which continues to the end of the chapter whose intent continues into the next chapter. It invites investigation.

We earthlings are possessed with a sense of insufficiency, impotency, and inferiority. Many of us have ringing in our ears unwelcome words like, "You'll never amount to anything! You won't make it!" We compensate by seeking to excel in performance or productivity, haunted by the feeling that we never quite made the grade.

But Paul assures us he is praying that we might become supernaturally aware of the incredibly great power of which we all who are saved have become recipients.

The Exceeding Greatness of His Power

I wish you would dwell on that phrase until it is indelibly engraved in your spirit. The word "exceeding" is the Greek word *uperballon* which means "throw beyond," "to surpass," or "to exceed." The word for "greatness" is *megathon* which is a derivitive of our very modern word "megaton" used to describe the destructive power of the atomic bomb. It is perceived to mean the destructive equivalent of one million tons of dynamite! Then there comes the word "power" from which we obtain the word "dynamite." The Greek word here is *dunamis.* What an explosive revelation this truth is going to be when you receive it!

There are five major words denoting some feature of power used in this matchless passage. They are:

Dunamis suggesting latent power,

Energia meaning expressed or reflected power,

Kratos indicating might or power in relation to the ability to gain an end or a dominion to be exercised,

Iskus referring to strength, as power in possession or ability to maintain, and

Exousias denoting authority or the ability to rule.

This is literally a power-packed passage. All these words are used to articulate what God wants every saint to know—namely that we are possessed with a power so fantastic that it raised Jesus from the dead and raised Him up to a position far above all levels of rule in the unseen realms. It is a *delegated* power—to us-ward who believe; it is a *demonstrated* power—it raised Jesus out of death and set him on high in authority. It is a *defeating* power—all things have been put under the feet of

Christ. It is a *dominating* power—He has been given Headship over all things in the Church. It is a *directed* power—it is for His Body the Church.

It is a power that belongs to us. We are both the recipients of it and the custodians of it. No other power than this satisfies the craving for power in the human heart. We were made to need, desire, and contain the power of God. Our insufficiency is forever overcome in this prayer's answer.

Do you see how these basic problems are solved?

THE PROBLEM OF INSECURITY . . . solved by the revelation of our calling from God and His guarantee, backed up by His sovereign power.

THE PROBLEM OF INSIGNIFICANCE . . . solved by the revelation of our being God's own treasured inheritance.

THE PROBLEM OF INSUFFICIENCY . . . solved by the revelation of His glorious power so great that it raised Jesus from the dead and gave Him authority over everything and everyone.

In coming to a sense of essential identity this prayer of Paul seems indeed to be a PRAYER YOU CANNOT LIVE WITHOUT.

9
The Romance of Redemption: What Has Happened?

Identity is a matter of record. History determines identity. We tend to reverse the right order and make our assumed identity determine our history of behavior. That history does not read well. The reasons for this are found in wrong assumptions which result in mistaken identity. Mistaken identity always results in wrong behavior or behavior out of accord with our true identity.

The romance of redemption, as a term used here, refers to all that is a matter of Divine record that has brought to us the privilege of being right with God and knowing Him as our God. It includes all that has been done in timeless eternity past, eternity future, and all in between. It embraces the Covenant made in the council of heaven between God the Father, God the Son, and God the Holy Spirit before there was time.

We are what or who we are because of what has happened in our behalf in *eternity past* and because of what has happened *to* us in time. All other matters pertaining to our identity pale into insignificance in the light of Who God is, what He has done, and is doing.

Let me put it another way. Whatever you and I are we are because of God, what He has declared, decreed, and determined. We are what we are because of what He has done. Our identity does not rest upon the unsettled sands of fate but upon the mighty power of a self-determining, sovereign God, Who has chosen according to the good pleasure of His will to do for us, to us, and in us what He has done! We get a feeling for this when we read what Paul shared in Ephesians 1:3-6:

> Blessed be the God and Father of our Lord Jesus Christ, who hath blessed us with all spiritual blessings in heavenly places in Christ: According as he hath chosen us in him before the foundation of the world, that we should be holy and without blame before him in love: having predestinated us unto the adoption of children by Jesus Christ to himself, according to the good pleasure of his will, to the praise of the glory of his grace, wherein he hath made us accepted in the beloved.

Now, for your own benefit, you might back off a moment and read that passage again, slowly and as objectively as you can. You can reach no other conclusion that this: "Something has gone on here!" And that "something" is all divine because, from its inception, no sinful minds were there to cloud it, and no sinful hands were there to mar it. It was done before time began.

In this chapter I want to ask and answer two vital questions: *One, what has indeed happened in our behalf preparatory to our salvation; and, two, what has happened to and in us in the personal processes of salvation?*

I am not aware of anyone ever doing for me what I will, in the following pages, attempt to do for you. I anticipate the gladness of being, myself, among the benefactors of this attempt. (In the next chapter I will attempt to summarize the answer to the central question of this volume: Who am I because of these truths?)

What Has Happened in Our Behalf?

My subject here must be considered in the light of the fact that I am dealing with a factor which is a total mystery to us on earth—namely the *timelessness of God.* Locked into time and space we mortals have little knowledge or appreciation of God's vantage point above and beyond our sphere. But in the realm beyond our "common cell" something has occurred that has radically affected our existence with which we had nothing to do. I will seek to reduce these considerations to a word where possible.

Foreknowledge

If God is, as we have declared Him to be, omniscient (all-knowing) we have to allow that He knows everything about everything and everybody. Though we are not comfortable with that, it remains absolutely true. This foreknowledge we mention here, however, relates not to a prior knowledge of things but to a prior knowledge of persons—you and me!

Think of it. You and I were in the mind of God a million years ago, yes, even countless aeons ago had time been measured by man. What was God thinking? What did He know about me? What standard or measure did He use in thinking of me? There are several similar statements that answer these questions:

> . . . to them who are the called *according to his purpose* (Rom. 8:28*b*).
>
> . . . according to the *good pleasure of his* will (Eph. 1:5*b*)."
>
> . . . according to his *good pleasure which he hath purposed in himself* (Eph. 1:9).
>
> In whom also we have obtained an inheritance, being predestinated *according to the purpose of him who worketh all things after the counsel of his own will* (Eph. 1:11)."

God was thinking of us in eternity past, and His thoughts were in accord with His own *purposes, plans, and pleasures.* This wonderful *foreknowledge* did not just involve information about us but a personal acquaintance with us. The term is " . . . *whom* he did foreknow . . ." (not "what"). The whole realm of His foreknowledge was on the grounds of His purposes and pleasures.

Predestination

The word here is *proridzo* and literally means to "mark off with a boundary beforehand." " . . . Whom he did foreknow, he predestinated to be conformed to the image of his Son." (Rom. 8:29)." Predestination is the determination of God beforehand based on His foreknowledge, which in turn, is based upon His own purposes and pleasure. It is likely that you will not only not understand this matter satisfactorily, you may have some serious questions about it. But may I gently exhort you to accept it as a biblically-supported fact that the true saints were known by God and predestinated in eternity past according to His good pleasure? You will then be free to enjoy now what you may not understand this side of heaven. We need to confess, "We were foreknown and predestinated."

Counted As Called

The Father saw us in ages past and counted us as called. (I refer to the saved.) He has decreed that "all things work together for them who love God, *to them who are the called according to his purpose*" (Rom. 8:28). This is called in theological circles the *effectual calling.* This does not refer to the universal appeal of the Gospel but to that which always results in the experience and state of salvation. Hence it is termed the *effectual* calling (so called because it culminates in salvation). " . . . Whom he did predestinate, them he also *called*" (Rom. 8:30). That this call is effectual is demonstrated by the fact that justification and glorification follow in sequence.

There is a reference to this calling in the universal sense in Matthew 22:14, "Many are called, but few are chosen" (this is *not* the effectual calling). Other passages which refer to the effectual calling are as follows:

> God is faithful, by whom ye were *called* unto the fellowship of his Son Jesus Christ our Lord. (1 Cor. 1:9)."

Wherefore the rather, brethren, give diligence to make your *calling* and election sure (2 Pet. 1:10).

For you see your *calling*, brethren, how that not many wise men after the flesh, not many mighty, not many noble, are called (1 Cor. 1:26).

To all that be in Rome, *called* to be saints (Romans 1:6*a*)."

You see, before we were here to hear we were counted as the called. And that calling was so effectual that it resulted in our salvation! Praise the Lord!

AUTHOR'S NOTE: I am not sure about you, but it is helping me to sit here and ponder the glorious truth that my identity as a child of God was determined in the mind of God in ages past. And . . . the rest is a matter of record!

Justification

Believe it or not, we are still discussing something that happened to us before we arrived here. Admittedly we entered into justification when we were joined to Jesus, but we were "counted righteous" in the court of heaven long before then. All the active verbs in Romans 8:29-30 are in the aorist tense which means "past." Hodge explains, "The aorist speaks of God who sees the end from the beginning and in whose decree and purpose all future events are comprehended and fixed."[1]

Justification means that we who are saved have been declared and recognized with all considerations of divine legality as righteous. The mystery facing all religions is in the question, "How can sinful persons be rightly related to Holy God?" The answer is that he cannot unless God chooses to do it by His own legal methods. Paul gives us that answer in Romans 8:33 and Romans 3:24:

It is God who justifies . . .

. . . being justified freely by his grace through the redemption that is in Christ Jesus.

The saved have no other claim to righteousness than here, but let it be known that the saved can claim righteousness here, giving all the glory to Jesus. John Murray in *Redemption Accomplished and Applied* says, "Justification is an act which proceeds from God's free grace. It is an act of God and of God alone. And the righteousness which supplies its ground or basis is the righteousness of God."[2]

In a succeeding chapter on righteousness and God's new creation we will discuss justification from a present point of reference.

Glorification

In point of time, from our vantage, this is future. From God's vantage it is accomplished. It essentially marks the time in which what began with the effectual calling climaxes in completion. The fact of eternity will become an event at the moment, when, in the fulness of time all the purposes of grace will be realized in every saved individual, as well as the whole Body of the saved of all time.

In the meanwhile, however, God views us as . . .

FOREKNOWN . . .
PREDESTINATED . . .
CALLED . . .
JUSTIFIED . . .
and
GLORIFIED!

This has happened for us who are saved. Now let us turn to another question that has heavy bearing on our identity:

What Has Happened in and to Us?

We now move from the objective to the subjective and to the event and processes of salvation. As glorious as are the objective facets of the truths of our salvation, nothing can compare with the miracle that God affects in us in the whole scheme of redemption.

Regeneration

As marvelous as the truth it conveys is the majesty of the word itself. The Greek word in Titus 3:5 is *palingenesia* from *palin* which means "again" and *genesis* which means "birth" or "beginning." Murray eloquently defines it: "God affects a change which is so radical and all-pervasive, a change which cannot be explained in terms of any combination, permutation, or accumulation of human resources, a change which is nothing less than a new creation by Him who calls all things that be not as though they were, who spake and it was done, who commanded and it stood fast. This, in a word, is regeneration."[3]

That which was wrought for us objectively by the counsels of heaven is now gloriously being realized in us as we are "born again," regenerated. This is not effected by anything we have initiated. It is all of grace and all of God. We are able to have faith because of the fact that the regenerative processes have begun. We are able to repent because regeneration has begun. Faith and repentance are necessary, but they are provided by the God who purposes regeneration. He who demands faith supplies faith. Faith and repentance unto salvation are always together. Saving faith is repenting faith, and saving repentance is believing repentance.

The greatness of the breach between God and mankind, caused by sin and the breadth of the disparity between what God is in His holiness and what He demands in His righteousness and what we can perform at our best, are spanned by His glorious masterpiece in regeneration. We cannot, this side of heaven, possibly assess or articulate the glories of His workmanship in us. Regeneration is but the spring from which all that attends our salvation flows.

Justification—an Experiential State

We have already viewed the objective features of justification. Suffice it to say here that what God legally declared in eternity past, He experientially constitutes in us when we are born again. He can declare us legally righteous because He, in fact, has constituted us righteous. "For he hath made him to be sin for us, who knew no sin; that we might be made the righteousness of God in him" (2 Cor. 5:17).

In justification our judicial status, so declared by the Judge of Heaven, becomes our experiential state through Jesus Christ.

"Justification is a constitutive act whereby the righteousness of Christ is imputed to our account and we are accordingly accepted as righteous in God's sight."[4]

Adoption

An immediate result of regeneration, of being born again, is that of adoption. God becomes our Father, and we become his children. He declares it so on the basis of regeneration. This is an interesting matter in the light of the fact that in regeneration we are "born again" into the family of God, and in adoption we are legally declared His children and are given the Spirit of adoption. "And because ye are sons, God hath sent forth the Spirit of his Son in our hearts, crying, Abba, Father" (Gal. 4:6).

Thus we have the best of both arrangements. We have been born by the power of the Spirit into the family of God and have also been adopted. The arrangement is both legal and practical, academic and actual, declared and dynamic.

Sanctification

The root word here is "holy". The meaning is "to cleanse and set apart for divine usage." The word "saints" is derived from this word—"holy ones." We can be holy because the Holy Spirit is within us as regenerate people. It is immediate, continuous, and ultimate. That is: the act is immediate, the process is continuous, and the perfection is ultimate.

Union with Christ

We have discussed this central doctrine in Chapter 8. Yet it seems incomplete not to mention it again here at the peak of the mount of redemption. Union with Christ is the central truth of the whole doctrine of salvation. There is no one truth which so immediately yields the reality of our true identity as our union with Christ. In this blessed union we have freedom from guilt, freedom from futility, and freedom from fear because we cannot think of the past, present, or future apart from our being in Him. We are in His past—thus, no guilt; we are in His present —thus, no futility; we are in His future—thus, no fear.

Before we leave this chapter let's summarized in chart form what we have discussed here.

WHAT HAS HAPPENED IN OUR BEHALF?

Foreknowledge
Predestination
Counted as Called
Justification
Glorification

WHAT HAS HAPPENED IN AND TO US?

Regeneration
Justification
Adoption
Sanctification
Union With Christ

In the following chapter we will come to basic conclusions about identity on the basis of what we have discussed here.

10

Being True to the New You: Do You Know Who You Are?

> Therefore if any man be in Christ, he is a *new creature* [creation]: old things are passed away; behold, all things are become new (2 Cor. 5:17).
>
> After those days, saith the Lord, I will write my law in their inward parts, and write it in their hearts; and will be their God, and they will be my people (Jer. 31:32).
>
> A new heart also will I give you, and a new spirit will I put within you; I will take away the stony heart out of your flesh, and I will give you a heart of flesh (Ezek. 36:26).
>
> For in Christ Jesus neither circumcision availeth anything, nor uncircumcision, but a *new creature* (Gal. 6:15).

All of these Scriptures speak of the same matter, a new kind of creation which the Life of God would inhabit here on this earth. Here is the most amazing phenomenon since the miracles of Christ's incarnation, resurrection, and ascension—a NEW CREATION, a human being inhabited by Divine Life. We have grown to be entirely too passive and unexcited about it. It is an unexplainable mystery sociologically or psychologically. It leaves the experts in the behavioral sciences wide-eyed and open-mouthed.

A new creation means new behavior.

Laws written in the inward parts (in the heart) usher in new codes of conduct and new ethical dynamics. A new heart guarantees a drastic change in conduct. It is no wonder that the devil does not want the Church to come into the knowledge of its corporate identity. It is no mystery that the enemy will go to all ends to prevent the individual believer's discovery of his true identity. A new day will dawn with such a discovery. The Body of Christ will come alive with God's life. Individual believers will begin to walk in resurrection power.

Our identity is determined by what He has done on our behalf and what He has done in and to us. Because of what God has done in Christ and continues to do and because of what He has done through the Holy Spirit and continues to do, we may be certain as to our true identity.

I list, with only brief comment, twelve biblical descriptions cogent to our identity. By the time we are through we should have a grip on who we are from God's point of view.

Children of the Father

The full significance of Jesus was as the Son of the Father. "And the Word was made flesh and dwelt among us, (and we beheld his glory, the glory as of the only begotten of the Father), full of grace and truth" (John 1:14).

God is referred to as *Father* no less than 245 times in the New testament, 100 of those in the Gospel of John. The identity of Jesus Christ was and is inseparably connected with His being Son to God, the Father. Over and over again this is featured. "For God so loved the world that he gave *His only begotten Son* . . ." (John 3:16). He lived in complete dependence upon the Father. In divulging the master secret of His life Jesus declared:

> Verily, verily I say unto you, the Son can do nothing of himself, but what he seeth the Father do; for what things soever he doeth, these also doeth the Son likewise. For the Father loveth the Son and sheweth him all things that himself doeth (John 5:19-20).

When Jesus prayed, He called God "Father":

> These words spake Jesus, and lifted up his eyes to heaven, and

> said, Father, the hour is come; glorify thy Son, that thy Son may also glorify thee (John 17:1).

Five more times in the prayer of John 17, Jesus addresses God as *Father*, referring to Him as "Holy Father" in verse 11 and "Righteous Father" in verse 25.

When Jesus was asked by the disciples to teach them to pray, He was clear that they were to pray to God as *Father.* "After this manner pray ye, our *Father* which art in heaven . . . (Matt. 6:9).

Most of the references to the Father in the Gospel of John come from the lips of Jesus either *about* God or *to* God as Father.

It is through Jesus Christ that we become sons (children) of God: "But as many as received him, to them gave he power to become the sons of God, even to them that believe on his name" (John 1:12).

What we are now and what we will be in the future are centered around the fact that we are sons (children) of God:

> Behold what manner of love the Father hath bestowed upon us, that we should be called *the sons of God,* therefore the world knoweth us not, because it knew him not. Beloved, now are we *the sons of God,* and it doth yet appear what we shall be: but we know that, when he shall appear, we shall be like him; for we shall see him as he is (1 John 3:1-2).

We are encouraged to make the most of this blessed Fatherhood:

> If a son shall ask bread of any of you that is a father, will he give him a stone? or if he ask a fish, will he for a fish give him a serpent? Or if he shall ask an egg will he offer him a scorpion? If ye then, being evil, know how to give good gifts to your children: how much more shall your heavenly Father give the Holy Spirit to them that ask him (Luke 11:11-13).

If the whole Gospel centralizes the relationship of the Father and the Son and offers through their pre-arranged Covenant sonship for us all, surely our being *children of the Father* forms an essential element in our true identity!

Citizens of the Kingdom

Jesus made it patently clear that with Him came the kingdom. "But if I with the finger of God cast out devils, no doubt the kingdom of God is come upon you" (Luke 11:20). This leaves the kingdom in its eschatological sense quite intact but makes us currently citizens of that kingdom. Back in Chapter 1 we saw in Hebrews 12:28 the word about our "receiving a kingdom which cannot be moved." In 2 Peter we read, "For so an source entrance shall be ministered unto you abundantly into the everlasting kingdom of our Lord and Saviour, Jesus Christ."

There are three elements that make up a kingdom: A King, a subject or subjects, and a domain. He is the King, we are the subjects, and wherever we are is the domain of that kingdom.

We, then, are not only children of the Father, our Father is the King!

Parties to the Covenant

We have already discussed this glorious arrangement that has much to do with our identity. It means even more now that we view our Covenant God as our Father and King of the kingdom, of which we who are saved are citizens.

The promises of that Covenant quite clearly guarantee that we will be "done over" from the inside and that God will be our God and we will be His people. Being parties to the Covenant means that He will remember our sins no more. It should be mentioned here that the significance of the blood of Jesus means more than the sacrifice which caused it to be shed. The blood of Jesus contained His very life; thus we are saved not just by His death, we are saved through His life! That life is the legal guarantee of the continuing validity of the Covenant. Read this encouraging coverage of the Covenant:

> How much more shall the blood of Christ, who through the eternal Spirit offered himself without spot to God, purge your conscience from dead works to serve the living God? And for this cause he is the mediator of the new testament, that by means of death, for the redemption of the transgressions that were under the first testament; they which are called might receive the promise of eternal inheritance (Heb. 9:14-15).

This glorious Covenant was our heritage as we were born into the Family of God.

Parts of the Body

Body, Bride, and Building: These three illustrations do much to mark the nature of our identity as believers in Jesus Christ and children of God. No one illustration can bear the enormous weight of the truth we are seeking to understand better. The multiple use of illustrations is always better because it is safer. The use of only one model may find that model collapsing under the weight of the truth it is used to convey.

Paul uses the illustration of the body to discuss the gifts and ministries given by the Holy Spirit. This discussion is found in 1 Corinthians 12.

> For as the body is one, and hath many members, and all the members of that one body, being many, are one body: so also Christ. For by one Spirit are we all baptized into one body, whether we be Jews or Gentiles, whether we be bond or free; and have been all made to drink into one Spirit. For the body is not one member but many. Now ye are the body of Christ, and members in particular (1 Cor. 12:12-14,27).

Members of the Body of Christ! Can you fathom that? We are part of Him, even as the very parts of our bodies are a part of us. We are inseparable. We are the means of His mobility in this world.

Members of the Bride

It is no secret that one of the clearest models of divine truth is that of the husband-and-wife relationship. We are informed in Ephesians 5:23, "For the husband is the head of the wife, even as Christ is the head of the church." After that profound discourse in Ephesians 5 on husbands and wives Paul wrote, "This is a great mystery: but I speak concerning *Christ and the church* (Eph. 5:32).

Jesus referred to Himself as the bridegroom in several illustrations and parables. Here are samples of them:

> Can the children of the bridechamber mourn, as long as the bridegroom is with them: but the days will come when the bridegroom will be taken from them, and then they shall fast (Matt. 9:15).

> The kingdom of heaven shall be likened unto ten virgins, which took their lamps, and went forth to meet the bridegroom . . . watch therefore, for ye know neither the day nor the hour when the Son of man cometh (Matt. 25:1, 13).

In the wondrous proceedings of Revelation 19, amid the four "Alleluias," we are implored by the heavenly multitude to . . .

> Be glad and rejoice, and give honour to him; for the marriage of the Lamb is come, and his wife hath made herself ready. And to her was granted that she should be arrayed in fine linen, clean and white: the fine linen is the righteousness of saints. And he saith unto me, Write, Blessed are they which are called unto the marriage supper of the Lamb. And he saith unto me, These are the true sayings of God (Revelation 19:7-9).

The late Paul Billheimer, a dear friend of mine, allowed me to read an unpublished manuscript regarding this matter of romance in God's universe. He wrote:

"God has designated the church as the Bride, the Lamb's wife. Do not denude these terms. Do not vitiate their heavenly connotation. Earthly marriage is the highest type of romantic relationship between Christ and His Church Bride that fully corresponds to the relationship of holy and righteous marriage partners. To doubt or dispute this is to unlawfully plunder the biblical figure of its clear and unmistakeable implication and meaning."[1]

Then, Billheimer launches into a discussion which leaves me breathless. He speaks about the implications of the marriage of the Lamb and His betrothed, their vows, their future, the coming adventure of their lives together, their blessed activity in union, and their boundless joy in wedded bliss. This celestial love relationship, he depicts, will continue forever engaged in the "increase of His government."

I must admit that he moves into a realm to which I am almost a total stranger, but I will also admit that I am no little bit excited about such prospects because I am a part of the bride! "Even so, come, Lord Jesus!"

Stones in the Building

Jesus was depicted by Peter in Acts 4:11 as "the stone which was set at nought of you builders, which is become the head of the corner." In his first epistle he touched the subject again:

> To whom coming, as unto a living stone, disallowed indeed by men, but chosen of God and precious, *ye also are lively [living] stones,* are built up a spiritual house, an holy priesthood, to offer up spiritual sacrifices, acceptable to God by Jesus Christ. Wherefore it is contained in scripture, Behold I lay in Sion a chief corner stone, elect, precious: and he that believeth on him shall never be confounded (1 Pet. 2:4-6).

In this important illustration we are all living stones fitted around Christ the Head of the corner into a building for worship.

New Creations

We have touched on this before but cannot make too much of it. What we are in our identities are "his workmanship created in Christ Jesus unto good works, which God hath before ordained that we should walk in them" (Eph. 2:10).

In 2 Corinthians 5:17 this illustration is individualized. "If any man be in Christ, he is a *new creature.*" To be in Christ is to be identified as a new kind of entity in which all things are new, the old having gone for good.

Peter's Four Descriptions (1 Pet. 2:9)

Chosen Generation

Whatever joy is derived in discovering our individual identity merges into an infinitely greater joy when we realize that we, as individuals, are parts of a glorious whole. In this case it is a "race," a "generation" of people drawn together by one compelling word—chosen. This means we were chosen as individuals to be parts of a race of people for eternal fellowship with God and one another.

A Royal Priesthood

This is a double designation which enhances our sense of identity. We are "kingly priests" and "priestly kings." Kings, by right of their essential identity, rule as a matter of living. Priests, by right of their essential identity, worship as a matter of living. What does this imply of us who are *a royal priesthood?* Simply that, by right of our essential identity, we rule and worship as a matter of living.

A Holy Nation

We are identified as a "holy ethnic group," *ethnos hagion.* We are a nation separated by God and set apart for special purposes. When someone asks you, "Are you holy?" you ought to consult what God has said before you give an opinion. He not only declares that you are holy but adds that you are a part of a massive spiritual nationality that is holy.

A Peculiar People

We need to look a little deeper into this one. The word "peculiar" in today's vernacular is suggestive of "weird" or "strange." This is hardly the connotation here. The word in the Greek is *peripoiesis* which means "an obtaining" or "an acquisition." Here it is to be taken as "God's purchased possession." We do not belong to ourselves, but to Him, who has acquired us for His own special purposes.

We should not leave 1 Peter 2:9 without allowing the purpose for which we exist to be noted: "That we should show forth the praises of him who has called us out of darkness into his marvelous light"

This, in a brief word, is *who we are and what we are for!*

Accepted in the Beloved

It is difficult to know both where to begin and where to end in a chapter like this. We may have reached the "mountain peak."

> According as has hath chosen us in him, before the foundation of the world . . . to the praise of the glory of his grace, wherein he hath made us *accepted in the beloved* (Eph. 1:4*a*,6).

Individually and corporately, we have been accepted in Jesus

Christ. Acceptable and accepted! If we knew nothing of all the other divine designations of our true identity and had only this one, surely we would have a reason to rejoice. With Him with whom we all have to do, before Whom we all must stand, we are accepted!

More than any other fact, I believe, Satan seeks to impugn this one. He is our accuser and avers that we have no standing with God, no acceptance in heaven, and no reason for feeling good about who we are! If, as I have previously declared, God has done what He declares He has done and we are what He declares we are, we are indeed accepted within the sphere of His Son, Jesus Christ. And there is nothing contingent about the acceptability and acceptance of the Son with the Father. In union with Jesus I am to the Father as accepted as He!

Let's view these together before we leave this chapter:

Children of the Father
Citizens of the Kingdom
Parties to the Covenant
Parts of the Body
Members of the Bride
Stones in the Building
New Creations
Chosen Generation
Royal Priesthood
Holy Nation
Peculiar People
Accepted in the Beloved

When you are feeling low, read this chapter again. Rehearse and celebrate your identity by repeating aloud what God in His Word has said about you. BE TRUE TO THE NEW YOU (now that you know who you are!)

11
Sin and God's New Creation

If the question hasn't yet come up, it should have. So, whether it has or hasn't, I raise it here.

The question to which I am referring is, "*If I am God's New Creation in my essential identity, why do I still have trouble with sin?*"

That question has not occurred to many simply because they believe that sin is so *indigenous* to the believer that it is *inevitable.* Before reading the next sentence, I want you to read the foregoing statement once again. Your willingness to set aside all preconceived notions, ideas, mind-sets, and human opinions is absolutely necessary for an understanding in the coming discussion. And I consider this discussion preconceived of such a vital nature as to stress that the whole message of who you are in Christ may indeed hinge on a proper perception of what we discuss here.

A Clever Deception

"Well, I just sin every day. Can't help it! That's just the way it is. After all, I'm just a sinner saved by grace."

Have you ever heard that statement or one similar to explain a recurring sin or defeat? Or perhaps, closer to home, *you* have made a statement like that. If you haven't spoken it aloud, you surely at best have thought it and at worst have been consumed by the futile feeling that it may be entirely true. I want to examine the statement with the confession that on the surface *it seems tragically all too true!* But the reason for its seeming truth is twofold: first, there is a mixture of truth in it; and, second, because of the power of an untruth so energized as to apparently prove itself true. Does that sound strange to your ears? Then let me make another statement which may shed some light on that claim:

> When you or I believe a lie, whether by simple passive consent or active confession, we give Satan legal room to take that lie, and our faith in it, and wrap it in a system of deceit that will make it look like, for all practical purposes, the truth.

So you recognize that, if the above statement is valid, much of what appears to be true in this clever deception is the result of our believing a lie and not because there is inherent truth involved. Because of the width and breadth of this clever deception, I am going to dissect it almost word for word.

"Well, I just sin every day. I can't help it!"

The first statement may indeed be true, but never is it true because of the second. Nobody sins (as a believer) because they can't help it! Get this through your brain and into the depths of your soul: *Not once, not one single time, since you have been saved, have you ever sinned because you had to, because you couldn't help it!* You were by nature a helpless sinner and of all such Jesus said, "Ye are of your father, the devil, and the lusts of your father ye will do" (John 8:44*a*). The confession (which heads this paragraph) is true of an unregenerate sinner. There is no recourse but to sin. The enemy would be all too glad if every believer were deeply certain that it is also true of us who are saved. But if we confess it, the enemy has a right to enforce the confession to such a degree that it looks as if it is true! Then what is proper to say and to think without being presumptuous or unscriptural?

"I don't have to sin all the time. I can help it!"

Is that statement too much for you? Then you need to know two wonderful facts:

1. A whole discourse in the Bible was written so we might not practice sin.

2. That same discourse informs us about what to do in case we do sin.

Now, hear that scripture: "My little children, these things write I unto you, *that ye sin not, and if any man sin, we have an advocate with the Father, Jesus Christ, the righteous.*" As usual the scripture closes the case!

"That's just the way it is. After all, I'm just a sinner saved by grace."

The statement is so common that few ever dare to protest it. That isn't the way it is because that isn't the way we are. Before we were saved we were by nature, choice, and behavior helpless sinners. However, something marvelous happened. God, in His glorious grace, gave us the twin gift of repentance and faith, with which we turned from our sin and to the Savior. He made us His new creations with the old passing away and all things made new. *We are not just sinners saved by grace we are new creations* (2 Cor. 5:17) *and God's workmanship created unto good works* (Eph. 2:10).

Then, what is the proper statement to make in the place of the untrue confession of futility?

"It doesn't have to be that way, because I have become new, a saint saved by grace!"

A Double Caution

Stay with me! *The possibility of sin is always imminent!* We will never, as long as we live in this body of flesh, be perfect and above sin.

Caution # 1: AVOID THE PITFALL OF PERFECTIONISM. Set it as your goal, but please know that it will be achieved ultimately and perfectly *only* when we shed this body of flesh by our death or His appearing. There is a book out with the fetching title *Tomorrow I'll Be Perfect.* It has nothing to do with our subject here but reflects a common desire within us all toward some future time when we will be through with the miseries of imperfection. Yes, tomorrow we will all be perfect when we see Him and will be like Him, having seen Him as He is!

Caution # 2: AVOID THE FOOLISHNESS OF FUTILITY. Like every other area of study, this one has a ditch on either side. In one ditch there is perfectionism and pride; in the other there is futility and desperation. In the meanwhile, on the way to being perfect, we do not have to wait in futile desperation. We are going on, reaching out, learning, and growing up. We are neither perfect nor desperate, just people under construction! "But we all, with open face beholding as in a glass the glory of the Lord, are changed into the same image from glory to glory. Even as by the Spirit of the Lord (2 Cor. 3:18)."

Some Legitimate Questions

"If I am a saint, why are there times when it is so easy to act unsaintly."

"If I am a new creation and old things have passed away and all things have become new, why do some of the 'old things' keep coming up?"

"What happens when sin occurs, and how may I guard against sin as a believer?"

"If I have been freed from sin, as the Bible says I have (Rom. 6:6-8), why do I seem at times to be in bondage to it?"

"If I am in union with Christ, why does it seem that I am a 'spiritual schizophrenic' at times?"

These and many other questions confront the serious student of the Christian life. The first response, in many cases, to these questions is to retreat from biblical claims to a more easily understood (and seemingly consistent) defeatism. In other words, if we are going to be defeated all the time, it is easier to develop a theological position consistent with that defeatism. But that is neither desirable nor necessary.

We will in substance touch upon the answers to these and

many other questions generated by these considerations in the pages to come.

Two Dangerous Fallacies and a Basic Tenet

I want to be careful here not to speak more than or less than the truth. Allow me to make a summary to which we can return as needed:

FALLACY # 1: So little happened to me at salvation that sin is inevitable.

FALLACY # 2: So much happened to me at salvation that sin is impossible.

BASIC TENET: That Which Happened to Me at Salvation Makes Sin Untenable, Intolerable, Irrational, and Inexcuseable, and Victory Over It Possible!

A REVEALING DIAGNOSIS

I live in a body.

I have a soul—mind, will, and emotions.

I am a spirit.

When I was born again my body was basically unchanged, my soul was much the same, but I came alive in my spirit which was dead. My appearance may be much the same physically, and my personality patterns unchanged, but in my spirit I now house the Spirit of the Living God.

My body is yet to be redeemed, now unredeemed. It has within all the programmed habits that were there when I was saved. All drives are esentially intact; all my drives survived my conversion. This was by divine design. My appetite, ambition, sex, approval, and all the rest of my drives remain to be reckoned with. The enemy's plan for our sin lies in the attempt to seduce us into getting our legitimate needs met in an illegitimate fashion. All drives being intact means that these will be channels of expressed righteousness or, when we succumb to temptation, channels of sin.

The dignity of the individual is based upon the God-given power of choice. To destroy that choice would be to destroy man's dignity as God's creation. The same avenues which open to sin in the human mind and body likewise open to righteous deeds and behavior. The potential propensities toward sin are but powers for good when harnessed by the Holy Spirit. Right choices, coupled with the indwelling power of the Holy Spirit, result in proper conduct and discovered personhood. The spirit-you is the real you. As the Spirit of God within the human spirit controls you and me, the result is God's authentic plan for mankind unfolded.

You and I must learn that when we sin, it is out of accord with our redeemed humanity. It does not fit. Sin does not belong. But how does it occur?

The continuing inclinations toward sin are identified as "the world, the flesh, and the devil." The world is a power outside us; the flesh is a power within us; and the devil is a person who seeks to surround us. It is perhaps the flesh that constitutes the greatest mystery. A biblical survey of the uses of the term would demand extensive time and space. Let me use the term "flesh" here as it indicates the human body, yet unredeemed, and the mind, yet unrenewed. Sin occurs when any combination of influences within this evil trinity—the world, the flesh, and devil—are allowed to have the dominant role within us.

Sin is not only rebellion against God, falling short of divine measurements and a violation of God's holiness, it is also behavior inconsistent with my essential identity as a new-creation person. The realization of the latter will crown the experience of repentance. Sin is a break in fellowship and a disturbance in communion with God. Relationship is not broken and union with Christ is still intact, but the flow of fellowship and communion ceases until sin is confessed and forsaken.

We have not seen all the truth about sin until we recognize that it is not only against the very nature of God but also against everything He had made us to be as new creations. He has created us to be holy and blameless, given us a new nature and a new name, united us with Christ, and written His law within us. Sin is a breach of our redeemed identities. In sin I am not only being untrue to God but to my new, redeemed identity.

The Expense of Sin in the Believer

Sin disrupts fellowship both with God and with fellow believers.

Sin gives the enemy a valid accusation and ground to do further damage to the believer.

Sin blurs the identity and thus cripples the believer's conduct and prayer life.

Because sin tends to make us unmindful of who we are it results in behavior which does not reflect our true identity as saints.

Sin stunts growth and gives room for the enemy to plant strongholds detrimental to ongoing spiritual life.

Sin neutralizes boldness in both prayer and witnessing and thus blunts usefulness.

Sin shortcircuits the system of communication between the believer and God, which weakens the believer both in work and worship.

Sin forms a distorted testimony to a watching world, confusing those who are open to visible proof of the credibility of Christianity.

Sin grieves the Holy Spirit and quenches His power in the believer's life.

Sin frustrates the angels assigned to minister to and for the heirs of salvation.

Sin breaks down the system of biblical priorities by causing the believer to be bogged down in worldly interests.

Sin in the life of the believer carries within itself its most immediate consequences but must eventually bring about the decisive disciplines of the Father upon His children.

Anything that so adversely affects our lives as believers

should be dealt with quickly and decisively. Thus we should know what to do when sin overtakes us.

What to Do When Sin Occurs

Though we have been enjoined in 1 John 2:1 not to sin, we have also been instructed that we have a lawyer, "an advocate," in case we do sin. When we become aware that we have sinned we are to contact our attorney immediately by confessing our sin. Jesus ably reminds us of His qualifications to handle our case. First, He is in Himself righteous. Second, He is on good terms with the Judge. Third, He has paid the debt for all my sin by His own death on the Cross.

We cannot have unconfessed sin in our lives and be filled with the Spirit at the same time. Thus, as we repent of our sin, confessing it to our Advocate, we are reaffirming Him as Lord and allowing Him to fill us afresh with the Holy Spirit, i.e., bringing our lives back under His control.

Paul's letters to the Corinthian church were loving but stern rebukes of their disorders in doctrines and conduct. He wrote in 2 Corinthians 7:8-11:

> For though I made you sorry with a letter, I do not repent: for I perceive that the same epistle hath made you sorry, though it were but for a season. Now I rejoice, not that you were made sorry, but that you sorrowed to repentance: for ye were made sorry after a godly manner, that ye might receive damage by us in nothing. *For godly sorrow worketh repentance to salvation not to be repented of:* but the sorrow of the world worketh death. For behold this selfsame thing, that ye sorrowed after a godly sort, what carefulness it wrought in you, yea, what clearing of yourselves, yea, what indignation, yea, what fear, yea, what vehement desire, yea, what zeal; yea, what revenge! In all things ye have approved yourselves to be clear in this matter."

Paul's report of the Corinthians' response to his confrontation is a classic example for all Christians everywhere. Their response to his confrontive epistle caused them sorrow of the right sort. That kind of sorrow led to repentance which, in turn, led to deliverance. Paul reminds us that there is a sorrow of the world, and that sorrow works death. Doubtless this kind of sorrow finds the offender grieved that the sin was detected and did not work out to his advantage. Such deliverance as referred to by Paul brought them to a position of strength and decisiveness in their own stand against sin. *They had cleared themselves in the matters on which Paul had confronted them.*

Confronting Offending Believers

Paul, in the Corinthian letters, sets such an example of confrontation that it deserves serious investigation. In my early days as a pastor I was faced with the necessity of decisive church discipline. Fellow believers had sinned, were unrepentant, and were continuing in sinful relationships. I sought to handle the matters in a thoroughly scriptural manner, and the procedures were carried out.

The sad feature of this, as I recall it, was that not one of the offending parties was restored and delivered from the sinful relationship. The procedure in itself was scriptural and could not have been improved. I confronted the offending parties as kindly and yet as sternly as possible. Not until I reread the Corinthian letter in the light of what I am calling New Creation truths did I recognize the issue. I want you to view it as I did.

My confrontation with the offenders was largely on the basis of how destructive and inexcuseable were their sins, of how grevious they were to God, and how disappointing to fellow believers. While each of these features was valid I had left out a most important issue which Paul made much of to the Corinthians. I want you to investigate this issue as I list some of the statements Paul made. As we view these, please keep in mind that Paul was in the process of a scathing confrontation on more than a dozen different problems within the Corinthian church, ranging from doctrinal disorders to sexual misconduct of a most perverted type. What a shock and surprise was mine when I began reading the 1 Corinthian Epistle in a new light. I have chosen a few references in that epistle and will comment on them briefly:

> Unto the church of God which is at Corinth, to them that are sanctified in Christ Jesus, called to be saints, with all that in every place call upon the name of Jesus Christ our Lord, both theirs and ours. Grace to you and peace from God our Father, and from the Lord Jesus Christ. I thank my God always on your behalf, for the grace of God which is given you by Jesus Christ; that in every thing ye are enriched by him, in all utterance, and in all knowledge; even as the testimony of Christ was confirmed in you; so that ye come behind in no gift; waiting for the coming of our Lord Jesus Christ: Who shall confirm you unto the end, that ye may be blameless in the day of our Lord Jesus Christ. God is faithful by whom ye were called unto the fellowship of his Son Jesus Christ our Lord (1:2-9).

Do you see what I see? Not a word, at the first, about their offenses! No fierce words of rebuke. No threats of reprisal. No attempt to drive them to further shame by recounting their offenses. These come later, but the significant matter here is what has come first.

Paul reminds them of their essential identity in Christ, saints, "sanctified in Christ Jesus" (V. 2). He greets them with grace and peace (V. 3). He thanks God on their behalf for grace given them by Jesus (V. 4). He expresses confidence in their enrichment by Jesus in speech and knowledge (V. 5).

And on he goes affirming them, informing them of his unshaken confidence of their final confirmation as blameless in the day of Christ.

Read further comments from Paul:

> But of him are ye in Christ Jesus, who of God is made unto us wisdom, and righteousness, and sanctification, and redemption (1 Cor. 1:30).

> For we are labourers together with God: ye are God's husbandry, ye are God's building (1 Cor. 3:9).
>
> Know ye not that ye are the temple of God, and that the Spirit of God dwelleth in you? (1 Cor. 3:16)."

These are further words of affirmation and identity. Not until chapter 5 does Paul engage in explicit confrontation. What is of immense import is that he lays a foundation for his confrontation by reminding them of who they are, what has happened to them, where they are going, and of their riches in Christ.

Instead of saying at first, "How terrible you are, and what a terrible thing you have done!" he seemed to be saying, "Look at who you are: saints, enriched in all speech and knowledge, temples of God; wise with His wisdom; righteous with His righteousness; sanctified with His sanctification; and redeemed by His redemption." Can you imagine the effect of that on the offenders?

Right before he exposes their sin Paul asked, "What will ye? shall I come unto with a rod, or in love, and in the spirit of meekness" (1 Cor. 4:21)?" His foregoing words of affirmation and confidence were proof that his choice was to confront them in love and meekness.

Indeed Paul would "let the hammer down" later and would not spare in the process. What is worthy of our memory is that the whole process of confrontation, correction, and deliverance was founded upon Paul's assessment of their essential identity. Paul was using *identity therapy.*

As I reassessed Paul's approach my memory drove me back to those cases of discipline I mentioned earlier. I was made to wonder how much more blessed might have been the outcome had I known of Paul's method of approach. I am not encouraging here the softening of judgment on sin. What I am advocating is that it be preceded by and pervaded by affirmation and identity, as well as love and meekness.

> Brethren, if a man be overtaken in a fault, ye which are spiritual, restore such an one *in the spirit of meekness;* considering thyself, lest thou also be tempted (Gal. 6:1).

As I was in the process of learning this new view of sin and confrontation, I was thrust into a situation of having to confront a brother who had fallen into sin. As I met him he was in the pit of gloom. He had failed again! I could have denounced him, reminding him of how he had failed God, his family, and others. But he already knew that. I began to use Paul's method, reminding him that he was a saint, a new creation, a temple of God, and that his sin did not fit, was untenable and intolerable.

I spoke softly, and even as I spoke he broke into weeping as profusely as I have ever seen anyone weep. The reminder of who he was and of God's love and affirmation caused him to deem his sin as more serious than ever. His godly sorrow was deep, and his repentance was real.

A Summary Conclusion

With a new view of you, your essential identity in Christ, will come a new view of everything. Sin seems more severe, less tolerable, and more to be avoided than ever. A new view of God and people, and how you can be related to them with new sensitivities, will be yours.

The story is told of a young lady in a foreign land who was heir to the throne of her kingdom. She was only a child and was acting every bit like the child she was. Her governness, in whose care she was, reacted to her misbehavior by shaking her and declaring, "Young lady, do you know who you are? You are the queen-to-be of this kingdom!" Whereupon the child came to her senses, straightened her body to its full height, and remarked, "Well, if that is who I am, I must surely behave like the queen I'm to be!"

Believer, do you know who are? Do you know that your name is written on the roles of heaven? Are you aware that your body is the temple of God? Don't you know that you are God's workmanship, His masterpiece created unto good works?

These realizations constantly before you will surely affect your ability to face and conquer temptation and to grow in the knowledge of the grace of God as His New Creation. If you are who He says you are, you should surely behave in accordance with your identity! And remember, *inherent in your essential identity is the capacity to behave accordingly!*

12
Righteousness and God's New Creation

Righteousness is the central issue of this chapter. When it is finished I want you, the reader, to have a view of righteousness such as you have never had before. I want you to know what it is and what it means that God is righteous. I want you to see Jesus as the Just One and the Justifier of all those who believe. *But most of all I want you to see rightousness as it relates to you as a New Creation,* giving you reason to stand before God unashamed and unafraid and to walk before the world in such a way as to show the world the Way in Jesus Christ. First, I want us to have a working knowledge of the meaning of a word that will occupy our attention for the next pages.

Righteousness Defined

The Hebrew for righteousness is *tsedek* which meant originally "stiff or straight." Actually the word cannot be adequately translated by any one English word. It signifies God's dealing with men under the ideas of righteousness, justification, and acquittal.[1]

The word *tsedek* is also used of a full weight or measure toward God in the spiritual sense. It is also used in the sense of rendering justice and making right.[2]

In the Greek language the word for righteousness is *dikaiosune* which means the character or quality of being right or just. It was formerly spelled "rightwiseness" which clearly expresses its meaning.[3]

The simple word "right" seems to convey the heart of the message of the word "righteous." It is the state of being right. Of course, this necessitates a *standard* of righteousness or "rightness." It is presupposed here that the only standard of righteousness is God Himself.

In fixing the proper definition in our minds it will help to link some New Testament words together. They are:

JUSTIFICATION (*dikaiosis*), a noun.

JUST (*dikaios*), an adjective

JUSTIFY (*dikaioo*), a verb

RIGHTEOUS (*dikaios*), same as "just"

RIGHTEOUSNESS (*dikaiosune*), already referred to

Now, I am not trying to force you into learning the Greek language nor do I intend to impress you with my elementary working knowledge of Greek. What I want you to see is: All the vital words above have *one* root from which they are derived. It is vital to this study to realize that "righteous" and "just" are synonyms and that the meanings of "justification" and "righteousness" are inseparable.

There is another interesting word with the same root as these. It is *dikaima.* Its three usages approach the matter from three different directions:

First, in Luke 1:8, Zacharias and Elizabeth were introduced as being righteous *(dikaios),* walking in all the commandments and ordinances *(dikaiomasin)* of the Lord—blameless. The word is used here as a "standard of right conduct."

Second, it is used to denote a verdict of acquittal. "For the judgment was by one to condemnation, but the free gift is of many offences unto justification" *[dikaioma]* (Rom. 5:16).

Here is inferred the clearing of all offences with the guilt involved on the basis of (1) God's grace revealed in Christ through His vicarious death and (2) the acceptance of Christ through faith.

Third, two verses later, in Romans 5:18 it is used in reference to a righteous act: "Therefore as by the offence of one judgment came upon all men to condemnation; even so by the righteousness [*dikiaomatos*] (literally "righteous act") of one the free gift came upon all men unto justification" [*dikiaomasin*] (as used in 5:16). When we use the words which pertain to righteousness we are not referring to what I think or what you think to be right but to a standard of righteousness which is as rigid and unbending as are the character and Word of God.[4]

Righteousness Demonstrated

It is clear that in the Old Testament the matter of righteousness was always related to Jehovah, His character, His Word, and His actions. Man was referred to as "righteous" only when his life and character took on the same characteristics as were evidenced in God.

In Jeremiah 23:16, as we saw earlier on in the book, the name of God as *Jehovah-Tsidkenu* comes into consideration. This is apparently a Messianic prophecy, introducing Jesus Christ as *The Lord our Righteousness.* He is but a visible extension of God.

God is *the* standard by which all conduct is and will be judged. He and He alone is the standard of righteousness.

> Thy throne, God, is for ever and ever; the sceptre of thy kingdom is a *right* sceptre (Ps. 45:6). (Some translations render it "the sceptre of thy kingdom is a sceptre of *justice.*")
>
> Righteousness and judgment are the habitation of his throne (Ps. 97:2 *b*)."
>
> The statutes of the Lord are *right* (Ps. 19:8).
>
> Therefore I esteem all thy precepts concerning all things to be *right* (Ps. 119:128).

When we speak of God as being righteous we are clearly declaring that there is perfect agreement between God and His character and His acts, since He is the standard for all men.

So, let me state emphatically that *God is righteous and demands righteousness on the part of those with whom He will fellowship and call His own.* The terms of that righteousness must be in total accord with His very character, Word, and work, and must meet the measuring standards of His total system of jurisprudence. In other words, whatever we are that is acceptable to God, is of necessity going to be *legal.* There can be no "fudging" or "moving of the margins."

This one issue, God's demand of righteousness, is the monumental question before us. In the Old Covenant this demand was made abundantly clear. In the law was a knowledge of sin. In fact Paul said, "Morever the law entered that the offence might abound" (Rom. 5:20 *a*). But the law had no solution for sin; it only exposed it as the problem. It was to be the New Covenant, sealed with the blood of Jesus, that both exposed sin and supplied the solution by proposing a total change in the inner man, making of him a *new creation.*

Job asked the vital question, "But how should man be just with God?" (Job 9:2). Bildad later asked it in a similar way, "How then can man be justified with God? or how can he be clean that is born of a woman?" (Job 25:4).

This demand for righteousness is derived from both the character of God as evidenced in His Word and work and from within man. The latter is a deep mystery solvable only in the light of traces of divine revelation resident in unregenerate man. Listen to the amazing passage that gives us this light:

> For therein (in the Gospel) is the righteousness of God revealed from faith to faith: as it is written, the just shall live by faith. For the wrath of God is revealed from heaven against all ungodliness and unrighteousness of men, who hold the truth in unrighteousness; *Because that which may be known of God is manifest in them; for God hath shewed it unto them.* For the invisible things of him from the creation of the world are clearly seen, being understood by the things that are made, even his eternal power and Godhead; so that they are without excuse (Rom. 1:17-20).

This "shred" of revelation within man has spawned most, if

not all, the religions of the world. Something within the heart of mankind desires an affinity with something or someone "out there." There is a sense of "not-rightness" and some faint desire to do whatever it requires to achieve this "rightness." There is one decisive difference between world religions and Christianity. Religion begins with man and seeks to work toward God or whatever is perceived as god, whereas Christianity begins with God as revealed in Holy Scriptures and works toward man. Thus there are clearly presented two opposing views of righteousness: (1) Man's contrived righteousness and (2) God's legally arranged and supplied righteousness. The tragic fact, in addition to this, is that much of Christianity is engulfed with a mentality akin to the Galatian problem in which righteousness by man's performance became an issue.

Now I turn to consideration of righteousness and the believer, the New Creation. We have laid a foundation for this discussion by observing God as totally righteous, and bound by His Own righteousness to demand righteousness of all who would be His. Without righteousness on our part, the kind that God requires and demands, there can be no favor, no fellowship, and no future with God. "Justice and judgment are the habitation of thy throne" (Ps. 89:14). To be a citizen of the kingdom of God one must be righteous. It is an issue we cannot avoid.

The Righteousness Question

Can mankind be just (or righteous) before God? If so, how can this be? To make it further interesting, let me ask, supposing you to be a declared believer in Jesus Christ, *Are you Righteous?* The typical answer is a no-answer such as, "It all depends on what you mean," or, "I'm afraid that's too deep a subject for me." In a congregation where there has been no teaching on this subject, not 5 percent of the crowd would own up to being righteous, while virtually 100 percent would quickly and unashamedly admit to being sinful.

We have mastered the "sin-consciousness" and have not even

experimented with "righteousness-consciousness." I am certainly not advocating ditching the former for the latter, but I am suggesting the happy possibility of a balance between the two. In fact, I am certain that a rise in the "righteousness-consciousness" would free us from such bondage that we would have good reason to have less "sin-consciousness." That reason is: the more conscious we are of Him, and thus our righteousness, the more we will be motivated to behave in a manner befitting righteousness. Sin-consciousness should always be brief and result in righteousness-consciousness. Tragically, the opposite seems to be true most of the time. We are called on often to confess our sins. I do not remember an invitation ever given to confess our righteousness.

You may disagree, but I hold the possibility that this issue, our righteousness-consciousness, may be among the greatest truths unveiled for the Church of the twentieth century. The Church has preached failure, sin, weakness, and unworthiness so long that we have a failure-conscious, a sin-conscious, a weakness-conscious, and an unworthiness-conscious constituency. For this reason we struggle with everything, including faith, the authority of the believer over the enemy, and all that relates to our true, essential identity.

I know of no point around which the enemy will more stubbornly persist than this one. Our hearts can see the truth, yet our tradition-affected intellects will fail to yield. Our righteousness in Christ, however, is real!

One who discovered this truth reports, "When I saw this truth of my righteousness in Christ, I said, 'No, this cannot be.' Sense knowledge could not register it. It had no way to understand it. It was contrary to all my experiences. I went back to the Word and read, 'Him who knew no sin God made to be sin *that we might become the righteousness of God in Christ*' (2 Cor. 5:21). By the new birth He had made me His righteousness. I surrendered to the Word. I yielded to it. I no longer questioned it. I said, *'If He has made me a New Creation, if He has made me out of righteousness and holiness of truth, I must be what He says I am, though I have never been taught it and have never understood it.*" He further reported that it changed his perception of everything and brought victory as nothing else had done before in his entire life.

Key Biblical Declarations

> For he hath made him to be sin, who knew no sin; that we might be made the righteousness of God in *him* (2 Cor. 5:21).

This passage declares two truths necessary for a complete salvation—Christ being made sin and our being made righteousness. We have little or no difficulty with the first, Christ becoming sin; we have little thought of the latter, our becoming righteousness. It is not ours to pick and choose. They are both true! As vital as it is to believe that Jesus became sin for us is the vitality of believing that we become the righteousness of God in Him! If He did, we have! We, then, have every right to say what God says about us, no more, no less: "I am the righteousness of God in Christ."

> But of him are ye in Christ Jesus, who is made unto us wisdom, and *righteousness,* and sanctification, and redemption (1 Cor. 1:30).

We have no doubts about the righteousness of Christ, but here we discover the extension of His righteousness to us. The key words are "*unto us.*' Thus we may testify, "Jesus Christ is my wisdom, righteousness, sanctification, and redemption. He and He alone is my claim to righteousness!" No wonder that verse is followed by this clause of purpose, "That, according as it is written, he that glorieth, let glory in the Lord" (1 Cor. 1:31).

> Yea, doubtless, and I count all things but loss for the excellency of the knowledge of Christ Jesus my Lord: for whom I suffered the loss of all things, and do count them but dung, that I may win Christ. And be found in him, *not having mine own righteousness, which is of the law, but that which is through the faith of*

> *Christ, the righteousness which is of God through faith* (Phil. 3:8-9).

Paul leaves no doubt about where he stands in this matter. He had righteousness, that righteousness which comes from God through faith. It had become that magnificent obsession for which he gladly suffered the loss of everything!

> For all have sinned and come short of the glory of God; being *justified* freely by his grace through the redemption that is in Christ Jesus: Whom God hath set forth to be a propitiation through faith in his blood, to declare his righteousness for the remission of sins that are past, through the forbearance of God; To declare, I say, his righteousness: *that he might be just, and the justifier of him which believeth in Jesus* (Rom. 3:23-26).

Paul goes on to speak of the exclusion of boasting because this righteousness is solely by faith without the deeds of the Law. We, then, have been "freely justified" or, if you please, "righteousized." In doing so, Jesus Christ has evidenced His own righteousness—all this that He might be *just* and the *justifier* of all believers. "For as by one man's disobedience many were made sinners, so by the obedience of one shall many be *made righteous*" (Rom. 5:19).

The word here for "made" is better clarified by the word "constituted." Justification is the declaration of one as righteous. The reason that one can be declared righteous is because he has, as this verse indicates, been *constituted* as righteous. "Therefore bring justified by faith, we have peace with God through our Lord Jesus Christ" (Rom. 5:1).

If we are righteous as we are claiming in these pages, then we have standing in the presence of God because we have peace with Him through Jesus. Righteousness, as it pertains to the believer, has been defined as:

THE ABILITY TO STAND BEFORE GOD WITHOUT SHAME, GUILT, OR CONDEMNATION.

There are, in fact, many other passages informing us of our

relationship to righteousness. How important it is that we confess openly what we know of His righteousness and ours.

The Validity of Confession

Few have ever realized the place that confession holds in the life of the believer. We are prone to forget that it was the key word in our regeneration experience. "That if that shalt *confess with thy mouth* the Lord Jesus, and shalt believe in thine heart that God raised him from the dead, thou shalt be saved" (Rom. 10:9). Confession is just as important a key in our continuing walk with God as it was in our first step of faith. That confession, as we are presenting it here, should contain at least three facets:

1. What God has done *for* us.
2. What God, through His Word and Spirit, has done *in* us.
3. What and who we are *in Christ.*

We must not stop short of this threefold confession. We must do it unashamedly and openly, as well as continuously. These confessions will lead us to realize what God can do through us with the Word in our hearts and on our lips.

We should master the art of confession, not merely any confession that comes to mind, but that which is in the Word of God. The writer of Hebrews gives us a hint as to how this might work:

> For he hath said, I will never leave thee nor forsake thee. So that I may boldly say, The Lord is my helper, and I will not fear what man shall do to me (Heb. 13:5-6).

"He hath said" should motivate us to say, "So that I may boldly say . . ." Our confession is built upon what God has said, and is therefore safe and secure. What God says He is, He is, and I should confess it boldly and openly. What God says I am, I am, and I should likewise confess it gladly. If God says it, I can and should speak in agreement with it. Thereby what is true legally and positionally will be true vitally and experientially

The reason that the majority of Christians, though they are earnest, are weak, is because they have never dared to confess who they are in Christ. What they must do is find what they are in the mind of the Father, how He looks upon them, and then confess it. This can be found in the Epistles. When you find this, you boldly make your confession of what the Word declares you are. Rember that your faith never grows beyond your confession. Your daily confession of what the Father is to you, what Jesus is now doing for you at the right hand of the Father, and what the mighty Holy Spirit is doing in you will build a positive, solid faith life. After a while you will find that Romans 8:37 is true: "Nay, in all these things we are more than conquerors." You will never be a conqueror until you confess it.[5]

Righteousness . . . Legal and Vital

What is ours is ours. God has declared it, and God's actions are always forensic, legal, by the book. However, simply because something is legal it is not necessarily vital or experiential. There are millions of dollars in unclaimed inheritances in the banks of America. Those fortunes legally belong to somebody, but they are not being experienced. That which is legal is not becoming vital. The same is true in the matter of our righteousness. We have been constituted as righteous in the legal court of divine jurisprudence. What God has constituted He has declared. What stands between what I am and have legally and my experiencing of it is *my claim of it, my confession.* Just as a lost heir may step forward and claim what the legal court has declared as his or hers, I may step forward with claim in hand and take possession of that which has been mine all along!

Legal righteousness is positional righteousness. Positional truth has been taken by some to mean *potential* truth, thus totally changing its meaning. If God affirms in His unimpeachable Word that I am righteous, He does it on the ground of a perfectly legal arrangement. Thus I am positionally righteous. But if I am to enjoy and reflect the value of that positional truth I must own up to it, claim it, and confess it. I do not confess it to make it true. *I confess it because it is true.* In my confession I am "banking on" the truth being precisely what God says—nothing more and nothing less.

Between what is factual and that becoming actual is my faith confession that what God has said is true, whether or not I understand it, whether or not I feel it, or whether or not anyone agrees with me!

Our Helper, the Holy Spirit

> And when he is come, he will reprove the world of sin, and of *righteousness,* and of judgment; of sin, because they believe not on me; of righteousness, because I go to my Father, and ye see me no more; of judgment, because the prince of this world is judged (John 16:8-11)

Had not Jesus added verses 9 through 11 we would be without some life-giving, life-changing truth. We have the fact at the outset that the Spirit will convict of sin, righteousness, and judgment. Had not Jesus explained further we would have mistakenly assumed that the Holy Spirit's coming meant we would be constantly haunted by the sight of our sin, His righteousness, and our coming judgment.

While conviction of sin is surely the work of the Holy Spirit, the one sin—as Jesus explains—that we will be convicted of is that of unbelief. Such conviction will not drive us to despair but to faith. The blessed Spirit never convicts us of sin to make us miserable but to deliver us from sin-consciousness to righteousness-consciousness.

Then, He convicts us of righteousness. Now hear this, "Because I go to my Father, and ye see me no more." I have passed that statement scores of times, never taking time to ask what it meant.

What I am about to tell you has changed and is changing my

life. Read carefully. From the time He began His public ministry Jesus had been the point of reference for righteousness. Had you been there in the land where He walked, lived, and ministered, and had asked anyone, "Where can I see true righteousness?" anyone knowing Jesus would have replied, "Find Jesus. He is true righteousness!" But now, He was preparing to leave, the only reference-point for genuine righteousness in this world, to be seen no more! What now, when people would seek the sight of genuine righteousness? He is there no longer after His ascension. Is there no righteousness on the earth to view? Yes, there is! The Holy Spirit will convict men of righteousness, not only Jesus', but theirs because of Him. After His leaving, He will be seen no more, but they are staying and, convicted of righteousness, *they* will be the reference-points of righteousness.

Until the Holy Spirit convicts you of sin, you will never be driven to believe. Until the Holy Spirit convicts you of righteousness you will never be motivated to confess it as your standing before God.

For good measure, the Holy Spirit convicts of judgment—not ours but that of "the prince of this world," a judgment which has already taken place. The verdict has already been rendered; the court has decided, and the culprit is sentenced. When the Holy Spirit convicts you of this you will have no fear or frustration of the enemy. Until the Holy Spirit convicts you of the fact of the devil's judgment you run the risk of constant defeat from the devil's deceit.

Convicted of the sin of unbelief, you will become a believer. Convicted of the fact of righteousness, His and yours, you will stand before God without fear, guilt, or condemnation. Convicted that the devil is under divine sentence and thus working on a "shortened chain," you will face him with demanding boldness instead of retreating fear. He is afraid of your confession! Make it now before God, the angels, the demons, and before the devil himself!

I am a believer!

I am a righteous believer!

I am master of the devil because I am in him who has mastered the devil!

I RULE AND REIGN IN LIFE BY ONE—CHRIST JESUS!

How Righteous Are We?

Peter Lord, a friend of mine, asked a congregation, "On a scale of one to ten, how righteous was Jesus?" He then asked, "On a scale of one to ten, how righteous are you?" The first is easy to answer. For some reason, the second is met with hesitation.

Dare I say that I am as righteous as Jesus? Even now, I feel compelled to qualify that! Yes, I may dare, because the righteousness which I have is that which has come, not from my own efforts, but as a free gift of God through faith in Jesus Christ. Of course, we in ourselves are not righteous. *But we are not in ourselves any longer.* We are in union with Him Who is Jesus Christ, the Righteous One! I no longer have the right to speak or think of myself in any other position than "in Him." If I answer the second question with any other than "ten" I am descending to my own righteousness which I have highly overrated. Mine is a "zero," and self-righteousness has dictated me to give myself more credit than I deserve. But if I have His righteousness, it is nothing short of perfect righteousness—a "ten"!

I hear the voices already beginning. "Dangerous doctrine!" "Semi-heresy!" And with this I sound for you and for myself a warning, as well as a declaration:

ANY TRUTH TREATED FOR LONG AS THE WHOLE TRUTH MAY PROVE AS DANGEROUS AS AN UNTRUTH. THEREFORE, TREAT ANY TRUTH AS ONLY A PART OF THE WHOLE BODY OF TRUTH TO BE KEPT IN BALANCE BY ALL OTHER TRUTH.

Balance this with a sensitivity to sin and the need for immediate repentance. Keep it in perspective that we will not attain unto perfection until we see Him and become like Him, seeing Him as He is! View it through the glorious over-arching doctrine of the sovereignty of God. But see it through the work of the Holy Spirit Who is taking the things of Christ and making them yours and mine. Confess the truth, the whole truth, and nothing but the truth.

You are what God says you are and as much as He says you are. You have what He says you have and as much as He says you have. You may confess it and proceed accordingly.

The Greatest Miracle

Do you believe in miracles? Of course you do! The strange thing is that when most of us hear the word "miracle" we think about miracles in the realm of nature, physical healing, or some otherwise unexplained phenomenon. I want to describe for you, aside from the miracles surrounding Jesus' birth, life, death, and resurrection, *the greatest miracle.*

Here is a sinner, a loathsome displeasure to God. Dead in sin and condemned in the Court of Heaven, he is guilty of repeated violations of divine law and is, in himself, lawless and helpless to do anything to change himself. If he lives, life will be futile. If he dies, judgment and hell will be inevitable. He is separated from all God's promises. Descriptives fail to depict the full measure of the tragedy of this life without God. He is guilty, filled with shame and fear, and is condemned.

But . . . something begins to happen! God's Spirit begins to hover over his sin-cursed soul, breathing the gift of repentance, a brooding sorrow over sin and sinfulness. That breathing births a faith, and there results a confession from the mouth of that awful sinner, "Jesus Christ is Lord of life and death!" And it happens—this wonderful miracle! Regeneration, and with it forgiveness, justification, favor, and peace with God. The great list of offenses against that sinner is marked "paid in full." He is registered in the court of heaven as *righteousness,* the very righteousness of God in Christ. Heaven is his final destination but also his internal makeup. He is changed forever!

And that sinner was you and I! And this miracle has happened to us. And in the glorious exchange we have become God's New Creations, the very righteousness of God in Christ.

A Closing Word from G. Campbell Morgan

I found this statement without really looking for it, a sort of serendipity, I suppose. I thought it worthy of your reading.

> The declaration that in the Gospel there is a revelation of the righteousness of God does not mean that the Gospel has revealed that God is righteous. That revelation antedated the Gospel. The declaration clearly means that the Gospel reveals the fact that God places righteousness at the disposal of men who in themselves are unrighteous. If you tell me that salvation is deliverance from Hell, I tell you that you have an utterly inadequate understanding of what salvation is. Unless there be more in salvation than the deliverance from penalty of sins and foregiveness of sins committed, then I solemnly say that salvation cannot satisfy my own heart and conscience. *Man may not obey it, but there in the depths of human conscience is a response to righteousness, an admission of its call, of its beauty, of its necessity. SALVATION, THEN, IS THE MAKING POSSIBLE OF THAT RIGHTEOUSNESS.*[6]

13
All That Is Ours As God's New Creations

Not only are we all that God says we are, but we have all God says we have. As God's new creations we are His children. As His children we are His heirs. As His heirs we are joint-heirs with Christ. Joint-heris are not equal heirs. Equal heirs share an equal amount. *Joint-heirs share the whole inheritance together.*

Most people today understand the processes of wills and inheritances. A person, while he or she is living, arranges a legal document with instructions for the disposition of possessions after death. In Hebrews such is called a "testament." When that person dies the will or testament is in force but not until that person dies. Upon the death of the testator the will is read, and the disposition of goods is made according to the will of the testator. In our case that was Jesus.

> And for this cause he [Jesus] is the mediator of the new testament, that by means of death, for the redemption of the transgressions that were under the first testament, they which are called, might receive the promise of eternal inheritance (Heb. 9:17). The Spirit itself beareth witness with our spirit, that we are the children of God; and if children, heirs; heirs of God, and joint-heirs with Christ (Rom. 8:16-17*a*)

In Hebrews 9:16-17 we are further informed that where a testament is, there must be the death of the testator. In our case that was none other than Jesus, Who is both testator and mediator of the testament. What a marvelous arrangement. But through His death, we who were heirs-apparent became heirs in reality. The will and testament were in force. Then Jesus came back from the dead to mediate in His resurrection life what he had validated in His death.

When you and I responded to the effectual call of God to salvation we confirmed our position as heirs of God and joint-heirs with Christ. How amazing that He Who named us in the will lives in us in the person of the Holy Spirit, to show us what we have, as well as prompting us to claim and appropriate our inheritances.

The Problem of Unclaimed Wealth

Let's suppose that you and I were informed through the mail that we had each been left a sizeable inheritance. For the sake of our illustration, let's suppose that it was $1,000,000. When you received your letter there was rejoicing in your home. Being informed that the money had been deposited to your account in your local bank, you made note of that in your checkbook. At the first opportunity you checked your balance against the bank's balance, and sure enough you were $1,000,000 ahead. Then you begin to make decisions in the light of your new prosperity.

You first give the tithe and then a healthy seed-gift to the causes of the Gospel. Debts are paid and then investments and savings are considered. Gifts to the poor are made with joy. Some of those special things you have always wanted to do, but could not quite afford, are now in your plans. It would be difficult to imagine that some vital changes in your life-style would not occur.

Now back to me. I received the same letter and was notified of the same arrangement. However, I have a questioning mind. *Why, I don't even know the name of the person writing the letter. How do I know this is not some hoax? I really don't deserve this. I did nothing to merit it. Why me?*

The result of this questioning was that I pitched the letter in the trash can and promptly forgot about it. My life went on at the level of my capacity to generate revenue. There was no change in my life-style. My account of my bank balance was unchanged. But the fact is the same deposit was made in my account that was made in yours. I simply disregarded the letter and made no note of it in my checkbook.

Do you see the situation? Same inheritance. Same arrangement. You gladly claimed it, believed it, acted upon it, and began living in appropriation of your inheritance. I doubted, forgot, and disregarded it, and nothing happened. And life goes on as it had before. Both of us are millionaires in fact. Both are legally wealthy, positionally rich. But yours is validated by belief, confession, and appropriation. Mine is static and useless, made so by unbelief, doubt, self-consciousness, and the refusal to claim the inheritance. Wealth that is stored and unclaimed is not wealth at all. That which is legal will not become vital until it is believed and acted upon. That which is positional will not become experiential until it is received by faith. That which is factual will not become actual until action and appropriation are mixed with trust.

The problem of unclaimed wealth is a dreadful tragedy in the Christian world today. People are living in spiritual poverty when, in fact, all that is needed for the living of a victorious Christian life is theirs by legal inheritance. But I am sure that we could become more specific and assume that the eyes perusing these pages belong to someone who is not living up to the inheritance that is yours. Let's try to solve that problem.

Our Executor

Jesus Christ, in the Person of the Holy Spirit, is both our Mediator and our Executor. This is a permanent arrangement. He knows the terms of the will and the size and magnitude of the inheritance. How sizeable is the inheritance?

> But as it is written, Eye hath not seen, nor ear heard, neither

> have entered into the heart of man, the things which God hath prepared for them that love him (I Cor. 2:9).

My paraphrase: *You cannot imagine what God has ready for you!* And since God knows that it is beyond your imagination He has made arrangements for that:

> But God hath revealed them unto us by His Spirit: for the Spirit searcheth all things, yea, the deep things of God . . . Now we have received, not the spirit of the world, but the Spirit which is of God; *that we might know the things that are freely given to us of God* (I Cor. 2:10,12).

Furthermore, Jesus informs us that the "the Comforter will teach us all things, and bring all things to our remembrance . . . (John 14:26). "He shall receive of mine, and shall shew it unto you. All things that the Father hath are mine; therefore said I, that he shall take of mine, and shall shew it unto you" (John 16:14*b*-15).

The Spirit knows how much is yours and mine. It is on deposit and can be withdrawn by faith through prayer. I will spend the rest of this chapter assessing and specifying our wealth.

General Statements of Our Declared Wealth

I will simply list without comment Scriptures that are pertinent with emphases on the pivotal words in each passage:

> Blessed be the God and Father of our Lord Jesus Christ, who blessed us with *all spiritual blessings* in heavenly places in Christ (Eph. 1:3).

> Therefore let no man glory in men. *For all things are yours.* Whether Paul, or Apollos, or Cephas, or the world, or life, or death, or things present, or things to come; *all are yours;* And ye are Christ's; and Christ is God's (1 Cor. 3:21-23).

> He that spared not his own Son, but delivered him up for us all, how shall he not with him *freely give us all things* (Rom. 8:32).

> Charge them that are rich in this world, that they be not high-minded, nor trust in uncertain riches, but in the living God, *who giveth us richly all things to enjoy* (1 Tim. 6:17).
>
> According as his divine power hath given unto us *all things that pertain to life and godliness,* through the knowledge of him that hath called us to glory and virtue (1 Pet. 1:3).

Let's look back over the emphasized words regarding our wealth. They look more impressive together than apart.

All spiritual blessings . . .
All things are yours . . .
All are yours . . .
Freely give us all things . . .
Who giveth us richly all things to enjoy . . .
All things that pertain to life and godliness . . .

Our Wealth Specified

Open your Bible to 2 Peter 1. We will honor his list of our riches. While there are many other passages we might observe, this list seems to be inclusive. In fact, my conviction is: There is not a need we have or can ever have which is not met within the reaches of these declared riches. The fantastic introductory statement which prefaces the listing of our wealth is:

> Whereby are given unto us exceeding great and precious promises: that by these ye might be partakers of the divine nature, having escaped the corruption that is in the world through lust (2 Pet. 1:4).

On the basis of what the above passage describes we are enjoined to examine our wealth and add "wealth to wealth."

Diligence Demanded

Our project demands effort which is nothing less than concentrated and active interest. The word here for "diligence" is *spoude* which means "earnestness, zeal, or care," and sometimes suggests being in a hurry about it. The large Greek word that follows *spoude* means "to bring in alongside" and denotes that we are to bring in alongside our relationship with God every ounce of determination we can possibly muster. So, call all your faculties into the considerations to follow. You will need them! Observe your wealth!

Add to Your Faith

I often ask a congregation if they have enough faith. The answer, unless they have been forewarned and foretaught, is always a sad movement of their heads sideways to indicate a negative. "Is there anyone here with as much faith as George Mueller?" I might ask. (Mueller of Bristol, England, you remember, ran an orphanage with hundreds of children—purely on faith.) That question, too, invokes a negative answer. Then the shocker: The Bible indicates that you have all the faith you need! Then there is that incredulous look as if to ask, "I have . . . what?"

This passage does not say, "Go get faith until you have enough." It says, "Add to your faith . . . " Would God tell us to add another thing to the first thing if we did not have enough of the first thing in the first place? Or is it that God has not been as informed as you are about your deficiency of faith? Had He known what you know He would have suggested, "Go get faith until you have enough." Isn't that ridiculous? And it looks more so in print! Since God has stated in His Word, "Add to your faith . . . " you may say, "I have sufficient faith to go on with God." If you do not confess that and claim it, you have no basis for believing that you have anything God says you have. Faith is the foundation of the whole superstructure of our wealth in Christ.

FAITH . . . OUR FOUNDATION

Add to Your Faith . . . *Virtue*

Faith, accepted as sufficient, becomes the means of "adding" to our wealth. The Greek word here is derived from a root meaning "to supply" or "to outfit." In this case a preposition *epi* is added and suggests accumulative force, "to add further supplies" or "to provide more than was expected or could be demanded."[1]

How rare and wondrous is this word "virtue"! It means moral energy, ethical dynamic. In classical times it meant the god-given power or ability to perform heroic deeds, whether in military, athletic, or artistic accomplishments. Aristotle held that it was right behavior or the median between two extremes. Let me reduce it to this simplistic definition: "Virtue is the ability to behave properly in every given situation."

In faith we add to our faith . . . virtue. If He says we have it to add, we may confidently add it. Now we have faith and virtue. What is apt to happen when we wake up to the fact that we have these two tremendous capacities? We will *believe* and *behave.*

VIRTUE

FAITH . . . OUR FOUNDATION

Add to Your Virtue . . . *Knowledge*

Do you have enough knowledge? If you answer on the basis of faith, your reply will be in the affirmative. On what basis do we lay claim to adequate knowledge? Try this Scripture on for size, "But we have the mind of Christ" (1 Cor. 2:16*b*). If you read the context in which Paul has written that, you notice he wrote in a previous verse, "He that is spiritual judgeth all things, yet he himself is judged of no man" (1 Cor. 2:15). Yes, we have the mind of Christ because we have Christ Himself living in us. "But we have this treasure in earthen vessels, that the excellency of the power may be of God, and not of us (2 Cor. 4:7).

He Himself is that Treasure in Whom is resident all the treasures of wisdom and knowledge (Col. 2:3). The structure of our wealth continues to build. We are not only now able to *believe,* having faith, and *behave,* having virtue . . . we can *be wise,* having knowledge!

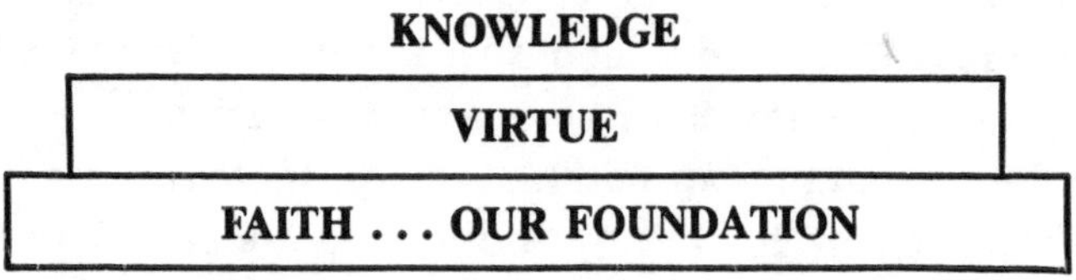

KNOWLEDGE

VIRTUE

FAITH . . . OUR FOUNDATION

Add to Your Knowledge . . . *Temperance*

How is your self-control? This word "temperance" used in the King James Version simply means "the ability to rule one's self." The Greek word is *enkrateian* with the root meaning "strength" with the preposition added, making it "inside strength." We are indwelt by the Holy Spirit who carries with Him adequate power. Thus we have the inside ability to control our wills under the operation of the Spirit of God.

Now we can believe, behave, be wise, and be strong!

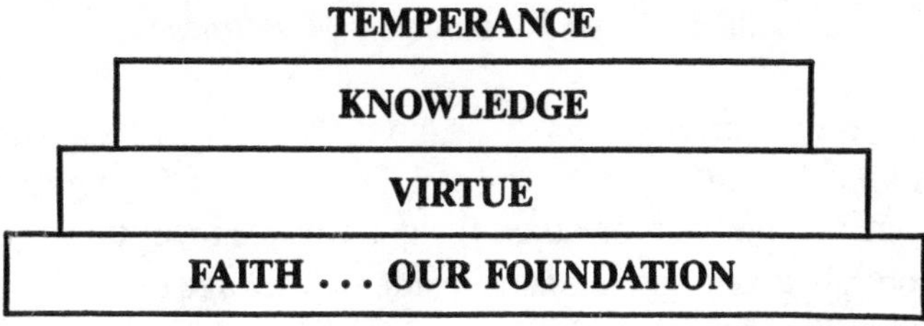

Add to Your Temperance . . . *Patience*

How blessed, yet illusive, this quality seems to be. Most of us have prayed for patience and have demanded it "right this minute"! Are you getting the drift of the matter and realizing that these qualities and powers are coming from Him and not us? We are adding them from His store, and His store is infinitely more than adequate! We may possess some of these qualities by human inheritance, but they are not adequate to measure up with God. These are supernatural qualities because they derive from His life.

The word here translated "patience" is *upomone* which means "abide under" and literally means the ability to "stand up under." He whose patience is unlimited has allowed us to partake in His very nature. Now we can believe, behave, be wise, be strong, and be steady!

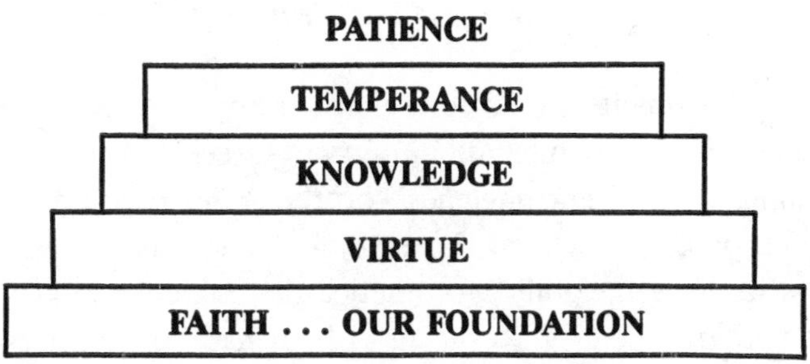

Add to Your Patience . . . *Godliness*

Do you perceive yourself as godly? Certain personalities seem kinder than others by nature. This often is deceiving, and a superficial piety is mistaken for godliness. Since the very life of God has taken up residence inside us we have every right to add "godliness." W. E. Vines observes that this word *eusebia* denotes a devoutness and piety which, characterized by a God-ward attitude, does that which is well-pleasing to Him.[2]

Now by adding wealth to wealth we have the capacity to believe, behave, be wise, be strong, be steady, and be devout!

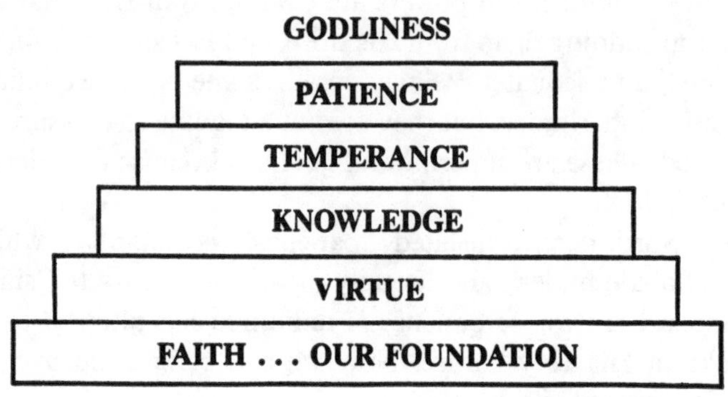

Add to Your Godliness . . . *Brotherly Kindness*

How this quality would surely hasten revival! It is the word *philadelphian,* a combination of two Greek words, *phileo,* meaning "to love" and *adelphos,* "brother." Since we are indeed blood-brothers in the New Covenant with one another and with Jesus, we have the ability to practice that which is in accordance with our identity. Regardless of our natural bent, we give in to our new identity to be lovers of one another. The addition goes on.

We can believe, behave, be wise, be strong, be steady, be devout, and be kind!

Add to Your Brotherly Kindness . . . *Charity (Love)*

And now we come to the crowning aspect of the life of wholeness. Isn't it interesting that what faith commences love climaxes, and all the other riches in between draw them together into a glorious whole.

And to think . . . you lived life so long leaning on your own qualities for victory, only to find out that they were yours in abundance in Him!

Diligence alone will walk us in the path from believing to be-loving! Concentrated effort and attention will be continuously needed under His Spirit's power.

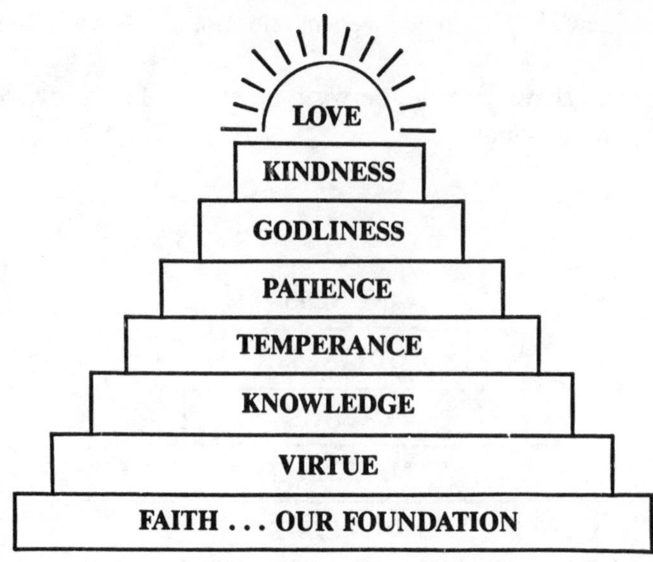

If Things Be in You and Abound . . .

The continuing presence of these qualities in you will mean that you will never be barren or unfruitful in the knowledge of Jesus Christ. Imagine such a state of being as this.

But He That Lacketh These Things . . .

But what is the case when these traits are not in evidence in us? The explanation follows in 2 Peter 1:9. "Ye are blind, and cannot see afar off, and hath forgotten that he was purged from his old sins."

A forgetfulness over what has happened is combined with spiritual myopia (short-sightedness) to rob us of a sense of identity which is in accord with God's Word and work. The principle prbves true again—the sense of identity tends to determine behavior. When we have no conclusive identity we lack the qualities God requires.

What Are We to Do?

If these things are lacking we should move into action immediately. For if we are not saved, we need to be saved. If we are indeed saved, then we need to put ourselves in order. "Give diligence to make your calling and election sure . . ." (2 Pet. 1:10 *a*).

There is the word "diligence" again. Knowing now that we are partakers of the divine nature and that we can begin on the foundation of faith, we begin to build a life by "adding." In so doing we are demonstrating the quality of life that confirms our election and calling. "For if ye *do* these things, ye shall never fail" (2 Peter 1:10*b*).

And here is a most important key . . . DO! You have faith—BELIEVE! You have virtue—BEHAVE! You have knowledge—act in the wisdom. The proof of faith is faith that works. Every one of these qualities is native to God's New Creation. Activate them! And the promise is—*you shall never fail*!

Entering the Kingdom

A glorious promise crowns this discourse in 1 Peter 1:11:

> For so an entrance shall be ministered unto you abundantly into the everlasting kingdom of our Lord and Savior Jesus Christ.

Discovering who we are and what we have, and acting accordingly, bear the immediate fruit of living under the Lordship of Christ and thus Kingdom living, if you please, LIVING IN KINGDOM COME!

Whatever it is to live in kingdom come, kingdom citizens are righteousness-conscious, power-conscious, and victory-conscious instead of sin-conscious, weakness-conscious, and defeat-conscious.

Allow the Holy Spirit to inventory your riches and report to you regarding all that is yours as God's New Creation.

14
Finding Out, Facing Up, Getting In, Going On

I am hoping at this stage of the reader's experience that the question is being asked, "If this is who I am, how do I validate the truth and move on with life?" or, "If this is my inheritance, how do I claim and appropriate it?" I have a slight aversion to formulas or procedures, but in this chapter I will go against that aversion to speak of steps toward practical implementation. You will see as we come to study Romans 6 that the procedures or steps are rather obvious.

Becoming Who You Are

In essence the matter of Christian growth is that of being conformed in belief and behavior to an essential identity. We are, as believers, what we are, whether we know it or not, believe it or not, or act like it or not. What we are is not what we feel ourselves to be or what the world claims we are. *We are what God says we are, not more or less.* We have what God says we have, not more or less. And God says what we are and what we have in His unimpeachable Word, the Bible. Jesus gave us a definitive word about becoming free in John 8:32: "And ye shall know the truth, and the truth shall make you free."

I am convinced that Jesus here is talking about more than correct factual knowledge when He refers to truth. He later declares, "I am the way, the truth, and the life" (John 16:1). It is not factual knowledge that sets us free. It is the knowledge of Jesus Christ as Truth and as presented in the Word of God.

Jesus puts it clearly in John 8:36, "And if the Son shall make you free, ye shall be free indeed."

Only the truth about who we are in Jesus Christ will lead us to the point where Christ can make us free. The occasion, as well as the instrumentality of this liberation, will be truths that describe Who He is in us and who we are in Him. When these truths are known, received, and appropriated, liberation always begins. As these truths are rehearsed, shared, applied, and implemented, freedom continues and grows.

When there is bondage at any point of the believer's life it is because these truths are either not known, or having been known, are not appropriated. Only a knowledge of the truth as it is personified in Jesus Christ has the dynamic to set us free.

He is Who He is, and He has told us Who He is in His Word. Whether or not He is to us Who He is will depend on whether or not we believe what He claims of Himself. And as we allow Him to become to us Who He is we will begin the adventerous journey of growing into who we are.

To express it another way, I have become a New Creation, created in righteousness, growing in Christlikeness, being changed by the Spirit of God into His image. I am, in fact, becoming *what I am.* What I am, I am in my spirit. As His Spirit in my spirit continues to control my being, my mind, will, emotions, and body are being changed. Thus, when He is allowed to take us over completely and exercise that dominance over us perpetually, we are becoming who we are in spiritual identity.

FOR TO ME TO LIVE IS . . .

With the recognition of the truth about our standing with God and our identity with Christ, and the commitment which ought to ensue, we will be able to assert with Paul, "For to me to live is Christ . . ." (Phil. 1:21). Until then it is inevitable that something else be allowed to shape our identities. We may be able to claim, "For me to live is riches, or fame, or power, or religion, or work, or pleasure." In any event, with these we find our identities in that to which we have given ourselves. Not until we give ourselves to Jesus Christ, to allow Him to reign without a rival in our lives, can we truly testify, "For to me to live is Christ." It is precisely at that point, where He becomes our very life, that our whole beings become the instruments of His expressed righteousness. "Being made free from sin, ye became the servants of righteousness" (Rom. 6:18).

Paul has put it in yet another light in Colossians 3:3-4: "For ye are dead, and your life is hid with Christ in God. When Christ, *who is our life,* shall appear, then shall ye also appear with him in glory."

Christ—our life! Imagine the connotations of that glorious truth. He is not only our Savior and our Lord, but desires to be the very Life of our life. He is our Life. What is our hope of living a life of complete trust in God? How can we anticipate hopefully the qualities of godliness being expressed through our lives? There is only one answer: *We cannot, but He can as He lives Himself in us.* And the fact is that all He did on earth, in His life, death, and resurrection, and all He is doing now in heaven, is working toward a Body filled with His life made up of individuals who have discovered Him as their life!

He is our life, and we have His life in us as a gift from God. It is vain for us to seek to copy the graces of His life without surrendering to His life within us. As we experience absolute surrender, dependence, trust, and obedience to His life within we will discover five basic truths about the Christ Life:

1. *It was a life derived from the Father.* He never forgot that fact or acted independent of it. It was the essence of His existence, the meaning of His personhood. He had no identity except the life of the Father. That life could only be maintained by the Father Himself. The totality of Christ's life was consumed in that identity, and that determined His purpose in life. "My meat is to do the will of him that sent me and to finish his work" (John 4:34).

2. *It was a life lived in dependence on the Father.* His life was not only one derived from God, but the principle of its dynamic came from God. Everything that He did and said, Jesus confessed, came as a result of what He saw and heard (see John 5:19,30). He never did a work because it seemed the human thing to do nor did He ever express a human opinion. Everything He saw God do, He did, and everything He heard God say, He said. For this reason everything He did was right, and everything He said was true. (The marvelous idea about this is that this is how He desires us to live!)
3. *It was a life laid down unto death that He and we might live unto God.* The paying of our sin-penalty is only a part of the significance of Jesus' death. What He died to do for us, He lives in us to perfect. Only as we come to identify with His death is He free to live His resurrection life in us. His life—our life.
4. *It was a life received again from the Father, a glorified resurrection life.* In essence Christ was born twice. The first birth was in Bethlehem and was a birth unto weakness. The second was a birth from the grave and was a birth unto glory. He was "the first-born from the dead" (Col 1:18). By giving up His life in weakness He received His life again in power and glory. In short, to receive the fullness of the expression of the Life of the Father Jesus must needs have given up his human life. That He did to reveal the glory of the life of God in us as individuals and in the Body of Christ, the Church. If we are to have the fullness of the Life of God in us we too must claim identity with Jesus' death. Thus we will not only be recipients but also channels of that continuing life.
5. *It was a life forever exalted with the Father.* Because Jesus laid down His human life in complete obedience, God has highly exalted Him and given Him a name above name.[1]

And everything that I have written of His life is true of your new life and mine, for His life is our life. We are participating day by day in His life, identifying with His commitment, communication, anointing, standing, and continuing work in behalf of mankind. Ours is not just some improved version of human life but His very life in us. The remainder of this chapter will describe an ongoing procedure by which the Bible declares that you and I can experience "grace reigning through righteousness unto eternal life by Jesus Christ our Lord" (Rom. 5:21).

In that verse the goal has been cited . . . grace so reigning through righteousness as to express itself in the highest form of life, eternal life. The problem was cited in Romans 5:20, "Moreover, the law entered, that the offence might abound. But where *sin abounded* [that is the problem—abounding sin] grace did much more abound." So we happily see that *abounding grace out-abounded abounding sin!* Now, let's plunge into the procedure.

Knowing . . . Finding Out

The last verses of Romans 5 should be read before beginning chapter 6. We left Romans 5 with the glorious prospects of abounding grace abounding over abounding sin and reigning through righteousness unto eternal life.

In the light of that brilliant prospect Paul asks, I believe by design, a perfectly absurd question. "What shall we say then? Shall we continue in sin that grace may abound?" (Rom. 5:1) Then shall we say . . . then? *When* we see the proposition presented in Chapter 5 of reigning grace! When this is seen I will say something, for such a prospect cannot be ignored. Then a question marks the apex of absurdity—"Shall we continue in sin that grace may abound?" It seems that Paul would almost have to study and research to come up with a question so off-the-wall! And yet as strange as it is, the apparent fact is that the greater proportion of Christians have answered, "Yes!" and have proceeded to a life-style that reflects it, and Christianity to them is a "drag."

Then there comes a shocking revelation in the form of another question. (Great teachers seem to have a proclivity for asking questions.) After seriously recoiling against his own question, "God forbit!" (or "Perish the thought!" or "No way!" or, as the Greek reads, "May it never be!") Paul asks, *"How shall we, that are dead to sin, live any longer therein?" (Rom. 6:2)* The question was asked in such a manner as to demand a negative answer, "We can't!"

Now, let's look at what Paul wanted us to understand:

Fact # 1. We died to sin. This fact does not wait on human understanding. We can't understand it. It does not wait on human emotion. We can't feel it. It does not wait on visibility. We can't see it. It is based on God's truth, what He has said about an already-accomplished fact!

A story was told about a fellow who was so distressed with life that he came to the conclusion he was dead. He announced the fact to his wife and friends and promptly dropped out of active life. Asked how he was, he would reply, "Dead, thank you!" His distressed family committed him to an institution for treatment, but he was none the better. Each day the doctor would make his rounds and ask him the same question, "How are you today?" The answer was always the same, "Dead, thank you." Nothing the doctor would say had any bearing on the man's mentality. He stubbornly persisted in his claim to be deceased.

The doctor thought of a project. He would prove once-and-for-all to the man's satisfaction that he was indeed alive. One day, in making his rounds, he asked the man, "Tell me, do dead men bleed?" The man thought a moment and replied, "No, dead men do not bleed!" The doctor then asked the man to extend his index finger and promptly pricked it with a pin. A bright, red drop of blood eased out of the tiny wound. The doctor expected that the problem would forever be solved, and the man would be convinced. But the man responded, his face filled with shock and surprise, "Well, I declare, dead men do bleed!" Many Christians are just as stubborn in the matter of the reality of their death with Christ. But it is indeed a fact, understood or not.

Fact # 2. We were buried with Christ by baptism unto death. (see Rom. 6:4) The second truth that we are to know is that our death is so complete we were "buried." A phase of life ended abruptly and another began. When things die you dispose of them—usually bury them.

This baptism is the substance of which water baptism is the shadow. Burial in water is the picture of our burial with Christ in death. When we were baptized into Christ at regeneration we were baptized into all that He experienced. When we think or speak of ourselves before our regeneration we are speaking of someone on the other side of death and burial. When the adversary accuses he is generally referring to what we were before we met Christ. His method is to bind us in thought and speech to the "old man" that was but is no more. We should agree with our adversary in the way and then be ready to account for ourselves as New Creation entities. "Yes, I agree that these things were true of me 'back when,' but it is no longer I that live, but Christ who lives in me. Now let me tell you about my new life: Jesus Christ is my Life!"

Fact # 3 We have been raised to resurrection life.

If we have been baptized into his death we have also been raised to walk in His life.

> For if we have been planted together in the likeness of his death, we shall also be in the likeness of his resurrection" (Rom. 6:5).

Again, we must be reminded that we are not discussing a life lived in attempted *imitation* of Christ but a life that is lived in *participation* with Christ. In beautiful believer's baptism we are depicting, not what happened to Him, but what happened to us because of what happened to Him. We are testifying in baptism, "Death has separated me from what I was. Burial has finished it. I am now a new creature walking with Christ in resurrection life."

Fact # 4 The old man (what I was before Christ), having been crucified with Christ, the body of sin is destroyed so that I need not serve sin. The word here for "destroyed" means "to make of none effect." The body of sin, or that spiritual superstructure within us as unregenerates that made sin inevitable, has been dismantled, brought to naught, rendered useless for practical purposes. Literally translated, this truth simply means that we don't have to be anymore the servants of sin. We have been given legal victory and freedom from it. We need not serve it.

Fact # 5 Sin and death have no more dominion over the believer. "He that is dead is freed fram sin . . . knowing that Christ being raised from the dead dieth no more; death hath no more dominion over him" (Rom. 6:7,9). Neither sin nor death has been removed from the picture; but the truth is that they have been deposed and no longer dominate us. Death has terminated that domination. Not everyone who has legal freedom is enjoying the blessings of experiential freedom. This reminds me of an appropriate illustration of this from my days on the farm. My father, at one time, raised a large number of pigs. There were big pigs, little pigs, middle-sized pigs—here a pig and there a pig, everywhere a pig. Now a pig is not your intellectual-type animal and has a simple interest pattern, namely, eating.

I remember, on occasion, when the winds came about harvest time, and much of our grain and corn was blown down, making it impossible to harvest by machine. My father came up with the idea of letting the pigs in after the machines had harvested what they could, allowing the pigs to pick up the waste. The problem was that the crop area was not fenced, and pigs were not interested in observing unseen property lines. The solution was an electric fence, an ingenious little device powered by an automobile battery, which sent electrical charges through a little wire about sixty times a minute. The little fence was put up and connected to the electrical device and turned on.

In itself it could never have discouraged a pig, much less keep it within bounds. But this did the trick. We turned the pigs into the area, and they went wild eating to their stomachs' content.

Their experiences with the electric fence were amusing. It would invariably happen one of two ways. They would be moving down the row eating everything in sight and suddenly come upon the little wire stretched across their path. Curiously they would touch the wire with the most sensitive spot on their nose. The result was "electrifying." You could hear the painful "oink" across the field. The curl in the pig's tail would straighten into an exclamation point as if in a display of sympathy or to convey alarm. But one fact for sure—the pig had forever "had it" with that fence. No sir, never again! The other encounter was one of total disregard. The pig would walk under the wire supremely preoccupied with eating. The wire would strike the pig in the nape of the neck, another sensitive spot. The spot was different, but the result was the same, straightened curl, painful "oink," and all. And the result was the same. Never again!

In fact, I believe, though we never proved it, had we turned the current off after all the pigs had been shocked, they still could have been contained with the sight of the wire and the memory of the shock. To carry it farther, I believe that so vivid was their memory and so settled their conviction that, had we drawn a line where the fence had been, they would have honored its memory. Dumb pigs!

But thousands upon thousands of believers are walking in the circumscriptions of sin, sin that long since has lost its power to control them. They have been freed but are still walking within parameters designated by sin's dominion over the old man. Freed but still shackled! Sin's dominion, long since broken, but in bondage still.

And death's dominion has been ended as well. We need not fear what can no longer do us harm. Yes, death is still around, thankfully so, but stands like a limousine waiting to transport us home when God is ready. But, thanks be to God, it no longer has dominion over us.

Let's summarize what we have come to know:

1. We have died with Christ.

2. We have been buried with Him.

3. We have been raised to walk in resurrection life.

4. We have witnessed the bringing to nought of the old man that the body of sin might be made of no effect.

5. Sin and death have no more dominion over us.

All this is true because His death was my death and His life is my life.

> There's a Man in the Glory Whose life is for me,
> He's pure and He's holy, triumphant and free.
> He's wise and He's loving, tender is He:
> And His life in the Glory my life must be.
>
> There's a Man in the Glory Whose Life is for me,
> He overcame Satan: from bondage He's free.
> In life He is reigning, Kingly is He;
> And His life in the Glory my life must be.
>
> There's a Man in the Glory Whose Life is for me,
> In Him is no sickness: no weakness has He.
> He's strong and in vigor, Bouyant is He;
> And His Life in the Glory My life may be.
>
> There's a Man in the Glory Whose Life is for me.
> His peace is abiding; patient is He.
> He's joyful and radiant, expecting to see
> His Life in the Glory lived out in me![2]

Reckoning . . . Facing Up

Now that we know certain truths we can turn to the next step—reckoning! The word simply means "to account as being so." It is the Greek word *logidzomai* from which we get our word *logic.* Reckoning is the exercise that renders the legal, vital; the positional, experiential; the factual, actual. It is the means by which we make the real, realized.

Unknown, unreckoned wealth is unrealized, and thus unuseful wealth. On the foundation of what we have witnessed in the previous discussion under *Knowing . . . Finding Out,* we are to reckon (or to account as being so) two basic facts:

1. We are to reckon ourselves to be dead indeed unto sin.
2. We are to reckon ourselves alive unto God through Jesus Christ our Lord (Rom. 6:11).

There is the mistaken notion abroad in the land that we reckon ourselves dead to sin in order to be dead to sin. Not at all! We reckon ourselves to be dead because God has said so. The reckoning does not make it true; it is already true. The reckoning seizes it, asserts it, and benefits from it. We do not reckon three and four to be seven in order for three and four to be seven. Three and four are seven if we never reckon it.

What reckoning is, in reality, seems to be best expressed by the term "facing up." Let's look at these major truths upon which we are to reckon:

Dead Indeed unto Sin

We have not died, nor has sin died, but something has happened between us. Our old man, sold under sin and dominated by sin, has been crucified. We have died to the dominating dynamic of sin. It has no right to rule us anymore. If a man dies while under the sentence of death, that sentence has no more effect on him. We have been united with Christ and have been made one with His death. If He has died, we have died. His death is our death judicially and legally. In the court of heaven our death has been recorded. There is no condemnation lodged against us. What is true can be correctly and legally reckoned as true, and life can proceed along the lines of that truth. He has said, therefore, I may boldly say, "I have died to sin. God said it. That settles it. Believe it. That settles it for me."

Alive unto God

Negative reckoning is not enough. "For in that he died, he died unto sin once: but in that he liveth, he liveth unto God"

(Rom. 6:10). Both His death and His life are vital. Two vital negative commands issue from this "living unto God": First, we are not to allow sin to reign in our mortal bodies; and second, we are not to yield our members as instruments unto unrighteousness (see Rom. 6:12-13*a*).

Thus, dual reckoning makes real to us what is already real in His Word and puts us in a position to begin seeing the truth in the present tense. Reckoning is no less than the facing up, on our part, to what is true.

Yielding . . . Getting In

This is where the contract is validated, where the rubber hits the road. Because we know what we know, we can reckon on that. We can then yield to what we reckon. If we are dead indeed unto sin, sin has no more dominion over us. We have no reason to yield to sin. If we are alive unto God, then we should yield ourselves "as those that are alive from the dead, and our members as instruments of righteousness" (Rom. 6:13 *b*).

Yielding forms the entrance to the living of the life with Christ. His commitment to the Father is our commitment. Jesus was committed to the will of the Father and to finish His work. Not one of His faculties was for private use. His life was "unto God,"

Paul makes crystal clear that whatever we yield oursleves to, we become a servant of. "Know ye not, that to whom ye yield yourselves servants to obey, his servants ye are to whom ye obey; whether of sin unto death, or of obedience unto righteousness. Being made free from sin, ye became the servants of righteousness" (Rom. 6:16,18).

Obeying . . . Going On

Yielding is to obeying what a step is to a walk. This life filters down into a walk. Human order is walking, running, and mounting up with wings like eagles. God's order is the opposite —mounting up with wings like eagles, running, and then walking—and walking and walking. People who don't understand this will stay with us in the mounting up and running but will tend to abandon us when the walking begins. It is sometimes romantic to yield, but the walk is the daily grind, the nitty-gritty. We find the word "obey" twice in Romans 6:16. This is the continuing curriculum of the saint. Expecting the sensational, the exotic, the romantic may leave us exasperated and frustrated. The record is that Enoch walked with God three hundred years. His total biography in Genesis 5 takes up less than sixty words. Isn't there more to the story? I am sure that we would be greatly stirred by the details of those three hundred years, but the main reminder is that because He and God agreed, they could walk together and they walked and walked and walked. It simply does not get any better than that.

Walking with God is not the means to something; it is the end—the something we seek. In order for the walk to continue, obedience is constantly demanded. In Amos 3:3 God asks, "Can two walk together, except they be agreed?" To walk with God is to agree with God on every detail. To agree with God on every detail is to obey God in every command. And this is the blessed secret of this life.

The process is continuous. We continue to know, reckon, yield, and obey. We have observed the finding out, the facing up, the getting in, and the going on, and that is how it is going to be the rest of our lives. Praise the Lord!

15
Implications of New Creation Truth

As we near the end of our space together I want to draw several implications from this amazing body of truth. So what does it mean? How will our believing it affect our life-styles? What are the major implications that issue from the fact that we are God's New Creations, established in righteousness? I will try to answer these questions from three vantage points.

The Vantage Point of Heaven

It has been suggested that if heaven ever had a holiday it must have been when the miracle occurred in the upper room. The hosts of heaven had their first look at God's New Creations. The Father saw them in Christ. The Spirit saw them as His special temples. Jesus saw them as Brothers and Sisters in Covenant, alive in His life. The angels saw them as new charges, with unlimited possibilities, and were sent to minister for them who are the heirs of salvation (see Heb. 1:14).

Jesus would be the New Creations' intercessor in heaven. The Holy Spirit would be the New Creations' intercessor within. The Father, in the Court of Heaven, would hear the prayers of the New Creations on a different basis than before. They would now pray in the name of Jesus, presenting all that He was, and God would answer on that basis.

The unveiling of God's New Creations there in the upper room must have marked a banner day in heaven. The long awaited masterpiece had a last been created. The "in-Christ" man, the "Christ-in" man came into being. At last, God's secret weapon, the New Man, the New Creation was unveiled!

As God at creation had spoken of Adam, "It is not good that man should be alone," and created a helpmate for him, He also willed that Christ have a helpmate. Watchman Nee worded it well:

> His purpose was to have a victorious Christ and a victorious Church, a Christ Who has overcome the work of the devil and a Church which has overcome the work of the devil. His purpose is to have a ruling Christ and a ruling Church. This is what God has planned for His own pleasure, and He has performed to His own satisfaction. Because God has desired to do it, it is done. God desired to have Christ, and God also desired to have a Church which is exactly like Christ. God not only desired that Christ should rule, but that the Church should rule together with Christ. Even in glory Christ will still need His helpmeet. In warfare Christ needs a helpmeet, and in glory He also needs a helpmeet.[38]

What God saw in these New Creations was His Son's helpmate or helpmeet. And Christ saw His Body with which He would continue to exercise victory over the devil which He had accomplished and established through His death and resurrection. He would be the Head of this Body through which He would continue His work unto completion.

Thus, the Lord of Hosts, the Hosts of the Lord, and all of Heaven looked with joyful awe on the works that the hand of the Lord had wrought . . . man in Christ, a New Creation!

The Vantage Point of Hell

If heaven had a holiday when the New Creation was unveiled, hell surely had a horror-day! And the hosts of hell looked on in stark terror as God's masterpiece made its debut. The devil knew that He had nothing in Jesus. "The prince of this world has nothing in me . . ." He had no legal ground, no accusation to lodge with the court of heaven. And now, as he viewed this New Creation, he knew equally well that he was no match for God's secret weapon. He has no legal part in us. The demons must have huddled together in dread at the prospects.

There is something that we need to understand here. God's purpose through Christ was "to destroy the works of the devil" (see 1 John 3:8*b*). If God were to deal with Satan, it would be quick and decisive. But He has chosen to do it legally through man. The old man could not conquer Satan. The New Man, Christ Jesus, could and did, and equipped the New Creation man to maintain that victory. He has imparted His life to His Body, the Church, made up of New Creations. The devil and the demons know all too well our essential identity in Christ. They shudder to think at what could happen in the world if the Body of Christ world wide ever discovered its true identity. Their work is to keep it a secret, hold it under wraps, shroud it in controversy. It is their only hope.

The demons behold the New Creations flanked by ministering angels and shrink back in frustration and fear. If only we knew of ourselves what even the demons know of us, we could shake the very foundations of hell.

The Vantage Point of Earth

There are so many considerations here I want to list with little comment the implications of New Creation truth from the viewpoint of Planet Earth.

1. *It forms the greatest safeguard in the midst of temptation.* How we behave under the attack of the tempter will heavily depend on how we view ourselves and our standing in heaven. Our view of God's view of us will serve as a steadying influence amid temptation.

2. *It is the greatest motivation to personal purity.* If we are what we are, and we know it, we will be more inclined to act accordingly. There is no better deterrent to sin than the realization of who we are in Christ and the accompanying dynamic of His life in us. In the church we tend to motivate purity by

negative methods—how bad sin is and how bad we are if we engage in it. The pleas in the Word of God to leave off sin are often couched in terms of our identity as if to insist, "Since you are who you are, act this way!" "Know ye not that ye are the temple of God, and that the Spirit of God dwelleth in you?" (1 Cor. 3:16). A stern warning follows in the next verse, but the warning is flanked on either side with identity language. "If any man defile the temple of God, him shall God destroy; for the temple of God is holy, which temple ye are" (1 Cor. 3:17).

The same is true in other places where caution is raised against sin. Apply this approach to 1 Corinthians 6:15-20 (I will emphasize the identity phrases):

> *Know ye not that ye are members of Christ? Shall I then take the members of Christ,* and make them members of an harlot? God forbid. What? know ye not that he which is joined to an harlot is one body? for two, saith he, shall be one flesh. *But he that is joined to the Lord is one spirit.* Flee fornication. Every sin that man does is without the body; but he that committeth fornication sinneth against his own body. *What? know ye not that your body is the temple of the Holy Ghost which is in you, which ye have of God, and ye are not your own? For you are bought with a price: therefore glorify God in your body and in your Spirit, which are God's.*

Paul, in warning against idolatry, inquired, "What agreement hath the temple of God with idols? For ye are the temple of the living God; as God hath said, I will dwell in them, and walk in them; and I will be their God and they shall be my people. Wherefore come out from among them and be separate, saith the Lord, and touch not the unclean thing . . ." (2 Cor. 6:16-17).

Do you see in these passages the identity truths applied, along with the warnings against sin? Surely such an approach would liberate us from legalism and motivate us to diligence in moral and spiritual integrity.

3. *It introduces the grounds upon which we can best have fellowship with all God's varied family.* It is impossible that a

people with divergent backgrounds, persuasions, personalities, and opinions should ever come together, stay together, and go forward together without some supernatural intervention. New Creation truths, who we are in Christ and Who He is in us, put the whole matter in another light. Since our problems with one another are along the lines of the flesh, we can give up on ever cooperating effectively in that area. God has the answer, "Henceforth know we no man after the flesh . . . Therefore if any man be in Christ, he is a new creature" (2 Cor. 5:16-17). Knowing each other in Christ and having a unity that is not of this world paves the way for fellowship and cooperation on the highest plane and forms a vehicle through which God can do His mighty work.

4. *It creates a perspective in the midst of which the common personal problems most of us face can be solved.* Most, if not all, of the major personal problems we experience have to do with identity. Allow me to name some of these with only a comment. As you read, make application to your own problem areas.

A. Self-worth . . . New Creation truths will establish a biblical sense of self-worth. We are God's very own treasures.

B. Rejection . . . These truths let us know that in Christ we have been ultimately chosen and accepted. "If God be for us, who can be against us?"

C. Inadequacy feelings . . . He [Christ] is in me and I am in Him. "I can do all things through Christ . . ."

D. Guilt . . . "There is therefore no condemnation to them who are in Christ Jesus . . ."

E. Weakness . . . "My (God's) strength is made perfect in weakness."

F. Fear . . . "Since God is my helper, I will not fear what man can do to me."

G. Proper self-confidence . . . "God shall supply all your need according to His riches in glory by Jesus."

H. Anger, jealousy, irritability, and the like. These arise

out of insecurities issuing from a lack of satisfying personal identity. They belong to the old life. "Old things are passed away, behold, all things are become new." We are told to "put off the old man and put on the new man created in righteousness and holiness (Eph. 4:22-24)

I. Trouble with self-discipline . . . The ultimate cure in this area is the Lordship of Christ and its implications in making us His disciples. In identity with Him is discipline.

5. *It would transform the marriage relationship and the home.* If family members would begin to view one another as God views them, there would be a revival in the home. Unconditional acceptance among family members would implement love in its highest expressions.

6. *It would bring victory in the experience of prayer.* Much of our praying is passive, hesitant, doubtful, and nonexpectant. This is generally due to a conscious or unconscious feeling of unworthiness on our part. We are coming to the Father as favored children with whose prayers He is delighted as we draw near in Jesus' name.

7. *It would facilitate faith as no other body of truth.* It is not our failure to believe how great God is that keeps our faith-quotient low—but improper feelings about ourselves. A biblical perspective on our personal identity and our standing with God would cause an explosion of faith!

8. *There would be a breakthrough in spiritual warfare.* A knowledge of who we are includes the assurance that victory is ours as God's New Creations over the devil and his demons. We are "more than conquerors" not because we are inherently strong in ourselves but because we are in Him that has conquered. For the devil to continue having damaging influence in our lives there is the necessity of keeping from us the truths of our essential identity. Once these are discovered, established, and maintained the enemy has lost a major foothold.

These are only a few implications of the truths that we have discussed in this volume. In these days when the slightest doctrinal difference seems to be grounds to destroy the fellowship in the name of "defending the faith" we need truth to bind brothers and sisters together. I am not talking about organizational unity but organic unity, unity of the faith. We all stand at different points around the huge circumference of truth.

None of us has it all. For balance we need each other. Our fellowship and cooperation can only be initiated and facilitated in a bond of powerful truth. The body of truth touched on in these pages will greatly help secure that beginning.

16
New Creation Confessions

In these closing pages I would leave you with a blessing that has proved to be of considerable help and encouragement to me. Since I have claimed here that our faith never rises above our confession, I have also determined that our confessions must not only be correct but constant. Our faith level is our living level. "The just shall live by faith (Rom. 1:17*b*)." Faith rises or falls on the basis of our confessions.

One day, far away from home and alone, I seemed to be enshrouded in a cloud of anxiety, uncertainty, and depression. I could not pinpoint the exact source of my problem, but the feelings had to do with my real standing with God. The more I thought, the more exasperated I became. At last I spoke to God these words: "I would really love to know what You think of me." The Lord began to communicate with my troubled heart, urging me to go to the Word as if saying, "I have already made clear what I think of you in my Word . . . read it!"

I was moved to begin reading what the Bible taught about saints and included myself in that crowd. I began to personalize the statements. My anxiety turned to excitement. I moved to a typewriter in my motel room and sat there for about six hours putting down what I share with you here. In most cases these statements are simply scriptures personalized for your use in confession.

A Pre-Confession Confession

"I am a believer. I believe that Jesus is the virgin-born Son of God who came to this earth to redeem us from our sins. I believe that He lived a life without sin and died in my place on the cross. I further believe that He arose with victory over death, hell, and the grave. He was seen alive by many, and later in view of His followers He was lifted up to heaven out of their sight. I have trusted in Him as my personal Savior and do now confess Him to be my Sovereign Lord. I am in Him, and He is in me in the Person of the Holy Spirit Whom Jesus personally sent as my Comforter.

"The devil has no place in me because I am in Christ, and he has no place in Him. I am in Him Who has all things under His feet, and nothing under His feet is over my head.

"What God says He is, He is; what God says I am, I am. What He says I have, I have. I will confess such, whether or not I feel like it. I reject and renounce any thought or feeling contrary to the Word of God and receive and declare to be true all that comes from the Word of God.

"I renounce all bondage in my mind and body and claim the Holy Spirit's filling and anointing as I make these confessions in accord with the Word and Spirit of God. I overcome the Accuser by the blood of the Lamb, by the words of this confession, and declare my terminal commitment to the death if necessary. Whatever God has said, I may boldly say . . . so I will speak what He speaks . . . in Jesus' Name, Amen."

NEW CREATION CONFESSIONS

> "For in Christ Jesus neither circumcision availeth anything, nor uncircumcision, but a *new creature.*"

1. I am a believer in Jesus Christ and my name is written in heaven. I rejoice in this. (Luke 10:20).
2. I have been given authority to tread on serpents and

scorpions and over all the power of the enemy, and nothing shall by any means hurt me. (Luke 10:19)

3. I am blessed when I am poor in spirit and have the kingdom of heaven. (Matt. 5:3)
4. I am blessed when I mourn and will be comforted. (Matt. 5:4)
5. I am blessed when I am meek and will inherit the earth. (Matt. 5:5)
6. I am blessed as I hunger and thirst after righteousness, for I will be filled to satisfaction. (Matt. 5:6)
7. I am blessed when I am merciful and will obtain mercy. (Matt. 5:7)
8. I am blessed when I am pure in heart and will see God. (Matt. 5:8)
9. I am blessed when I am a peacemaker and will be called a child of God. (Matt. 5:9)
10. I am blessed when I am reviled, persecuted, spoken against falsely, and rejoice in gladness that my reward is great in heaven. (Matt. 9:10-12)
11. I am the salt of the earth and can influence the world for good. (Matt. 5:13)
12. I am a light in the world and can let my light shine and glorify God. (Matt. 6:14-16)
13. I can pray to the Father in secret, and He who sees in secret will reward me openly. (Matt. 6:6)
14. I lay my treasures up in heaven where they cannot be destroyed by man or time. (Matt. 6:20)
15. Since my treasure is in heaven, my heart is in heaven. (Matt. 6:21)
16. I don't have to worry about my life because God takes care of me. (Matt. 6:25-30)
17. I choose to seek God's kingdom and His righteousness first, knowing all the details of my life will be handled by God. (Matt. 6:33)
18. If I ask, it will be given; if I seek, I will find; if I knock, it will be opened unto me. (Matt. 7:7-8)

20. I choose to speak right words because I know that I will give account of every idle word I say. (Matt. 12:36)
21. I choose to speak right words because by my words I will be justified or condemned. (Matt. 12:37)
22. If I pray with another in harmony with God on anything, He will give it to me. (Matt. 18:19)
23. Whereever I am with another one or two, Jesus has promised to be there in the midst. (Matt. 18:20)
24. If I believe, all things are possible. (Mark 9:23)
25. I will not live by bread alone but by every word of God. (Mark 4:4)
26. If I give, it will be given to me, good measure, pressed down, shaken together, and running over. With the same measure that I give, it will be given to me again. (Luke 6:38)
27. I seek the Kingdom because it is the Father's good pleasure to give me the Kingdom. (Luke 12:31-32)
28. I am determined to bear His cross and thus be His disciple. (Luke 14:27)
29. I have received Him and have been given the power to become a child of God because I have believed on His Name. (John 1:12)
30. My purpose in life is to do God's will and work. (John 4:34)
31. I will to know the truth, knowing it will make me free. (John 8:32)
32. If Jesus makes me free I will be free indeed. (John 8:36)
33. He is the Vine; I am a branch; His Word cleanses me and prepares me for more fruitfulness. (John 15:1-3)
34. If I abide in Him and His words abide in me, I can ask what I will, and it will be done. (John 15:7)
35. I did not choose Him, but He chose me and ordained that I bear fruit and that fruit will remain. (John 15:16)
36. The Spirit has come to live in me, and He will teach me all things and guide me into all truth. (John 16:13)

37. Jesus has prayed and is praying for me now. (John 17, Heb. 7:25)
38. I belong to God, and Jesus is glorified in me. (John 17:10)
39. I am protected by the power of His name. (John 17:11)
40. I have His joy in me in full measure. (John 17:13)
41. I am kept from the evil one. (John 17:15)
42. I am one with all others of God's children. (John 17:21)
43. I have been given the glory of God. (John 17:22)
44. Jesus is in the Father; the Father is in Jesus; I am in Him; and He is in me. (John 14:20, 17:21)
45. I am one with the Father and Jesus the Son. (John 17:24)
46. I am God's gift to Jesus. (John 17:26)
47. I have received power since the Holy Spirit has come upon me and will be a witness to the world. (Acts 1:8)
48. "I am not ashamed of the gospel of Christ, for it is the power of God unto salvation, to everyone that believes." (Rom. 1:16)
49. I have been justified through faith. (Rom. 5:1)
50. I have peace with God through Jesus Christ. (Rom. 5:1)
51. I have access into God's grace wherein I stand. (Rom. 5:2)
52. I have reason to exult in sufferings. (Rom. 5:3)
53. Sufferings train me to endure. (Rom. 5:3)
54. Endurance brings proof that I have stood the test. (Rom. 5:4)
55. This proof is ground for certainty in me. (Rom. 5:5)
56. God's love has been shed abroad in my heart. (Rom. 5:5)
57. "Being justified, we [I] shall be saved from wrath through Him." (Rom. 5:9)
58. I have been reconciled to God through Jesus' death. (Rom. 5:10*a*)
59. I am being saved by the life of Jesus Christ. (Rom. 5:10b)
60. I have received the gift of God's grace. (Rom. 5:17)
61. I have received the gift of God's righteousness. (Rom. 5:17)

62. Through the obedience of Jesus I have been constituted as righteous. (Rom. 5:19)
63. I have been acquitted of all sin through Jesus Christ. (Rom. 5:19)
64. God's grace has immeasurably exceeded my sin. (Rom. 9:20)
65. God's goal and mine for me is that grace may reign through righteousness unto enternal life through Jesus Christ. (Rom. 5:21)
66. It is impossible for me to continue to persist in sin. (Rom. 6:2)
67. I have died to sin with Christ. (Rom. 6:3)
67. I have been baptized into Christ. (Rom. 6:3)
68. I have by that baptism been united with His death. (Rom. 6:3)
69. I have been buried by baptism with Christ. (Rom. 6:4)
70. I have been raised with Him to walk in newness of life. (Rom. 6:4)
71. I have been united with Christ in death and resurrection. (Rom. 6:5)
72. My old man (the man I used to be) was crucified with Christ. (Rom. 6:6)
73. My body of sin (the entity which made sin inevitable) was destroyed (put out of action). (Rom. 6:6)
74. I do not have to serve sin any longer. (Rom. 6:6)
75. I am dead indeed to sin. (Rom. 6:11)
76. Being dead to sin, I am alive to God through Christ. (Rom. 6:11)
77. I may now forbid sin to reign in my mortal body. (Rom. 6:12)
78. I may now put my whole being at God's disposal. (Rom. 6:13)
79. Sin shall no longer be my master. (Rom. 6:14)
80. I am not under law but under grace. (Rom. 6:14)
81. Being set free from sin, I have become a servant of God. (Rom. 6:22)

82. My members are instruments of righteousness. (Rom. 6:13)
83. I have fruit unto holiness and eternal life. (Rom. 6:22)
84. I have the gift of eternal life. (Rom. 6:23)
85. I thank God that He shall deliver me from the body of this death. (Rom. 7:24-25)
86. There is no condemnation to me in Christ. (Rom. 8:1)
87. I have been set free from the law of sin and death. (Rom. 8:2)
88. The righteousness of the law is fulfilled in me as I walk according to the Spirit. (Rom. 8:4-5)
89. I am not in the flesh since God's Spirit is dwelling in me. (Rom. 8:9)
90. He gave life to my mortal body through His Spirit. (Rom. 8:11)
91. I am led of the Spirit of God, being a son of God. (Rom. 8:14)
92. I have received the Spirit of adoption, crying, "Abba, Father" (Rom. 8:15)
93. His Spirit bears witness with my Spirit that I am His child. (Rom. 8:16)
94. I am an heir of God, a joint-heir with Christ. (Rom. 8:17)
95. As I suffer with Him, I shall also be glorified with Him. (Rom. 8:17)
96. My sufferings are not to be compared with the glory that will later be revealed. (Rom. 8:18)
97. I have the firstfruits of the Spirit. (Rom. 8:23)
98. I eagerly await the redemption of the body. (Rom. 8:23)
99. I eagerly await with perseverance. (Rom. 8:25)
100. The Holy Spirit helps my infirmities. (Rom. 8:26)
101. The Holy Spirit makes intercession for me according to God. (Rom. 8:26)
102. All things work together for my good. (Rom. 8:28)
103. God foreknew me. (Rom. 8:29)

104. He predestinated me to be conformed to His image. (Rom. 8:29)
105. He called me with an effectual call. (Rom. 8:29)
106. He justified me. (Rom. 8:29)
107. He glorified me. (Rom. 8:29)
108. If God is for me, who can be against me? (Rom. 8:31)
109. He has freely with Christ given me all things. (Rom. 8:32)
110. I and God's love are inseparable. (Rom. 8:35)
111. In everything I am more than a conqueror through Him. (Rom. 8:37)
112. Christ is the end of the law for my righteousness.
113. Believing in Him, I shall never be put to shame. (Rom. 10:11)
114. My feet are beautiful because I preach the Gospel. (Rom. 10:15)
115. I have reason to glory in Jesus Christ in all things that pertain to God. (Rom. 15:17)
116. The God of peace shall shortly crush Satan under my feet. (Rom. 16:20)
117. Grace and peace have come to me through God and Jesus. (1 Cor. 1:3)
118. I have been enriched in everything in utterance and knowledge. (1 Cor. 1:5)
119. He will confirm me to the end that I may be blameless in the day of Christ. (1 Cor. 1:8)
120. I have been called into fellowship with God's Son. (1 Cor. 1:9)
121. The Gospel is the power of God unto me. (1 Cor. 1:18)
122. Jesus is made unto me wisdom, righteousness, and sanctification, and redemption. (1 Cor. 1:30)
123. It is beyond my imagination what God has prepared for me. (1 Cor. 2:9)
124. God has revealed this to me by His Spirit. (1 Cor. 2:10)
125. I have received the Spirit that I may know the things that are freely given me from God. (1 Cor. 2:12)

126. I have the mind of Christ. (1 Cor. 2:16)
127. I am one of God's fellow-workers, a part of His garden, His building. (1 Cor. 3:9)
128. I am the temple of God whose Spirit lives in me. (1 Cor. 3:16)
129. All things are mine—the saints, the world, life, death, things present and future. I am Christ's, and He is God's. (1 Cor. 3:22-23)
130. I am already full, already rich, and reign as a king. (1 Cor. 4:8)
131. We (the saints) shall judge the world. (1 Cor. 6:2)
132. We (the saints) shall judge the angels. (1 Cor. 6:3)
133. I am washed, sanctified, and justified in the name of the Lord Jesus by the Spirit. (1 Cor. 6:11)
134. My body is a member of Christ. (1 Cor. 6:15)
135. I, joined to the Lord, am one spirit with Him. (1 Cor. 6:17)
136. My body, the temple of the Holy Spirit, is not my own. (1 Cor. 6:19)
137. I have been bought with a price, therefore I glorify God with my body. (1 Cor. 6:20)
138. My head is Christ. (1 Cor. 11:3)
139. I as a man am in the image of the glory of God. (1 Cor. 11:7)
140. I have been baptized into His Body by one Spirit. (1 Cor. 12:13)
141. I have been set in the Body as a member as it has pleased God. (1 Cor. 12:18)
142. I have need of the other members of the Body. (1 Cor. 12:22-23)
143. If I suffer, others suffer; if I am honored, others are. (1 Cor. 12:26)
144. God has appointed my position in the church. (1 Cor. 12:28)
145. In Christ I have been made alive. (1 Cor 15:22)

146. God is giving me the victory through Jesus Christ. (1 Cor. 15:27)
147. I can be steadfast, immoveable, always abounding in the work of the Lord. (1 Cor. 15:58*a*)
148. My work in the Lord will not be in vain. (1 Cor. 15:58 *b*)
149. God comforts me in all my tribulations. (2 Cor. 1:4)
150. As sufferings abound in me, consolation abounds in Him. (2 Cor. 1:5)
151. I am sealed by God through the gift of the Holy Spirit. (2 Cor. 1:22)
152. I am always led about in Christ's triumphal procession. (2 Cor. 2:14*a*)
153. I am made a fragrance of His knowledge everywhere. (2 Cor. 2:14*b*)
154. I am a sweet-smelling fragrance to God. (2 Cor. 2:15)
155. God has made me a sufficient minister of the New Covenant. (2 Cor. 3:6)
156. My sufficiency is from God. (2 Cor. 3:5)
157. The Spirit being in me, I have liberty inside. (2 Cor. 3:17)
158. I have received the ministry of the Gospel. (2 Cor. 4:1)
159. I have this treasure (Jesus Christ) in an earthen vessel (my body). (2 Cor. 4:7)
160. All things that happen to me are for my sake that grace may spread and thus cause thanksgiving. (2 Cor. 4:15)
161. I do not lose heart, due to the fact that my inward man is being renewed day by day. (2 Cor. 4:16)
162. My troubles are light and short-lived, working for a glory far greater than they. (2 Cor. 4:17)
163. I have a building not made with hands, eternal in the heavens. (2 Cor. 5:1)
164. I am confident, knowing that as long as I am in the body, I am absent from the Lord. (2 Cor. 5:6)
165. I walk by faith and not by sight. (2 Cor. 5:7)
166. I am confident and well-pleased to know that to be

absent from the body is to be present with the Lord. (2 Cor. 5:8)

167. I make it my aim, whether present or absent, to be well-pleasing to Him. (2 Cor. 5:9)
168. I am a new creation in Christ Jesus. (2 Cor. 5:17)
169. Old things have passed away. (2 Cor. 5:17)
170. All things have become new. (2 Cor. 5:17)
171. I can now know people after the Spirit and not after the flesh. (2 Cor. 5:16)
172. I have been reconciled to God through Jesus Christ. (2 Cor. 5:18)
173. I have been given the ministry of reconciliation. (2 Cor. 5:18)
174. I have been given the message bf reconciliation. (2 Cor. 5:19)
175. I am an ambassador for Christ beseeching men to be reconciled to God in Christ's behalf. (2 Cor. 5:20)
176. Jesus Christ became sin for me. (2 Cor. 5:21*a*)
177. I have been made the righteousness of God in Him. (2 Cor. 5:21*b*)
178. He became poor that I, through his poverty, may become rich. (2 Cor. 8:9)
179. If I sow bountifully, I will reap bountifully. (2 Cor. 9:6)
180. God is able to make His grace abound to me and as a result I have a sufficiency in all things all the time. (2 Cor. 9:8)
181. As a result of this there is a sufficiency to every good work. (2 Cor. 9:8)
182. My seed sown will multiply to my enrichment. (2 Cor. 9:11)
183. This will result in further liberal giving which will result in many thanksgivings to God. (2 Cor. 9:11)
184. I walk in the flesh, but I do not war after the flesh. (2 Cor. 10:3)
185. My weapons are not carnal, but spiritual, mighty in God. (2 Cor. 10:4)

186. I am able to pull down strongholds, cast down arguments, and high things liften against the knowledge of God, and bring thoughts into the captivity of Christ. (2 Cor. 10:4-5)
187. God's grace is all I need for sufficiency. (2 Cor. 12:9*a*)
188. I can rejoice in infirmity. (2 Cor. 12:9*b*)
189. I have the power of Christ resting on me. (2 Cor. 12:9 *c*)
190. I can take pleasure in infirmities, reproaches, necessities, persecutions, and distresses. (2 Cor. 12:10*a*)
191. God's strength is made perfect in my weakness. (2 Cor. 12:9)
192. When I am weak, then I am strong. (2 Cor. 12:10*b*)
193. I have been delivered from this present evil age through the death of Christ. (Gal. 1:4)
194. I have been crucified with Christ. (Gal. 2:20)
195. The life I am living is not mine but Christ's. (Gal. 2:20)
196. I now live by the faith of Him who loved me and gave Himself for me. (Gal. 2:20)
197. I, being of faith, am a child of Abraham according to covenant. (Gal. 3:7)
198. I, being of faith, am blessed with Abraham. (Gal. 3:9)
199. I have been redeemed from the curse of the law that the blessing of Abraham might be mine in Christ. (Gal. 3:13-14)
200. I am a son of God by faith in Jesus Christ. (Gal. 3:26)
201. Being baptized into Christ I have put on Christ. (Gal. 3:27)
202. I am of Abraham's seed, an heir according to promise. (Gal. 3:29)
203. I am no longer a servant, but a son, an heir of God through Christ. (Gal. 4:7)
204. I can stand fast in the liberty wherewith Christ has set me free and will not be entangled again with the yoke of bondage. (Gal. 5:1)
205. Having the Holy Spirit, I have all His fruit—love, joy,

peace, longsuffering, kindness, goodness, gentleness, faithfulness, self-control. (Gal. 5:22-23)

206. The world has been crucified unto me and I unto the world.(Gal. 6:14)
207. I am a new creature in Christ Jesus, thus neither circumcision nor uncircumcision prevails. (Gal. 6:15)
208. As I walk according to this rule, peace and mercy are upon me and upon Israel. (Gal. 6:16)
209. I am in Jesus Christ. (Eph. 1:1)
210. I have received grace and peace from God and Jesus. (Eph. 1:2)
211. I have been blessed with all spiritual blessings in heavenly places in Christ Jesus. (Eph. 1:3)
212. I have been predestined to adoption by Jesus according to the desire of God. (Eph. 1:5)
213. I have been chosen before the foundation of the world to be holy and without blame before Him in love. (Eph. 1:4)
214. I have redemption through His blood, the foregiveness of sins. (Eph. 1:7)
215. I have received all wisdom and prudence aboundingly. (Eph. 1:8)
216. He has made known to me the mystery of His will. (Eph. 1:9)
217. I have obtained an inheritance. (Eph. 1:11)
218. I am predestinated according to His purpose Who works all things according to His own desires. (Eph. 1:11)
219. I have been sealed with the Holy Spirit of promise. (Eph. 1:13)
220. The Holy Spirit is the Guarantor of my inheritance. (Eph. 1:14)
221. I have the Spirit of wisdom and revelation in the knowledge of Him. (Eph. 1:17)
222. The eyes of my inner man have been enlightened. (Eph. 1:18*a*)
223. I know the hope of my calling. (Eph. 1:18*b*)

224. I know the riches of the glory of His inheritance in the saints. (Eph. 1:18*c*)
225. I know the exceeding greatness of His power. (Eph. 1:19)
226. All things are under his feet; I am in Him; all things are under my feet as well. (Eph. 1:22)
227. Having been dead, I have been made alive. (Eph. 2:1)
228. I have been raised up with Jesus and now sit with Him. (Eph. 2:6)
229. I have been saved by grace through faith, that faith itself being a gift from Him. (Eph. 2:8)
230. I am God's workmanship (handiwork) created in Christ Jesus unto good works. (Eph. 2:10*b*)
231. God has before ordained the works that I should walk in. (Eph. 2:10)
232. Once afar off, I am now made near by the blood of Christ. (Eph. 2:13)
233. He is my peace and has abolished all enmity contained in the law against me. (Eph. 2:15)
234. I have full access through Jesus to the Father. (Eph. 2:19)
235. I am a fellow-citizen in the household of saints. (Eph. 2:19)
236. I am being built together with the saints into a habitation of God in the Spirit. (Eph. 2:22)
237. I am a fellow-heir and a partaker of His promise in Christ. (Eph. 3:6)
238. I have boldness and access with confidence by faith in Him. (Eph. 3:12)
239. I am strengthened with might by His Spirit in the inner man. (Eph. 3:16)
240. I know the love of Christ which passes knowledge. (Eph. 19*a*)
241. I am being filled with all the fulness of God. (Eph. 3:19 *b*)

242. He is able to do abundantly above all that I ask or think. (Eph. 3:20*b*)
243. This is all according to His power which is now working in me. (Eph. 3:20*b*)
244. I will one day be a perfect man, unto the measure of the stature of the fulness of Christ. (Eph. 4:13)
245. I do not have to be tossed about by every wind of doctrine, by the trickery of men, and their cunning craftiness. (Eph. 4:14)
246. I can speak the truth in love and grow up in him unto all things. (Eph. 4:15)
247. I have chosen to put off the old man. (Eph. 4:22)
248. I have been renewed in the spirit of my mind. (Eph. 4:23)
249. I have chosen to put on the new man which was created according to God in righteousness and holiness. (Eph. 4:24)
250. I once was darkness, but now am light in the Lord. (Eph. 5:8*a*)
251. I am able to walk as a child of light. (Eph. 5:8*b*)
252. I choose to be strong in the Lord and the power of His might. (Eph. 6:10)
253. I choose to stand and put on the whole armor of God. (Eph. 6:13)
254. I accept the armor piece by piece: Righteousness, truth, the gospel of peace, the helmet of salvation, the shield of faith, truth as a belt. (Eph. 6:14-17)
255. With the shield of faith, I can quench all the fiery darts of the wicked one. (Eph. 6:16)
256. He who started a good work in me will finish it on time. (Phil. 1:6)
257. I will be ashamed in nothing, but with all boldness will magnify Christ in my body. (Phil. 1:20)
258. For to me to live is for Christ to live. (Phil 1:21)
259. It was given to me to believe on Christ and to suffer for His sake. (Phil. 1:29)
260. The mind which was in Christ is in me. (Phil. 2:5)

261. God is working in me both to desire and do His good pleasure. (Phil. 2:13)
262. My citizenship is in heaven from which I eagerly await His coming. (Phil. 3:20)
263. He will transform my body to be conformed to His glorious body. (Phil. 3:21)
264. I can rejoice in the Lord always. (Phil. 4:4)
265. I don't have to be anxious for anything. (Phil. 4:6*a*)
266. I choose to pray about everything with thanksgiving. (Phil. 4:6*b*)
267. I will make my requests known unto the Lord. (Phil. 4:6)
268. The result of this will be that God's peace will guard my heart and mind in Christ Jesus. (Phil. 4:7)
269. I can do all things through Christ who keeps on strengthening me. (Phil. 4:13)
270. God is now meeting all my needs according to His riches in glory in Christ Jesus. (Phil. 4:19)
271. I am being filled with the knowledge of His will in all wisdom and spiritual understanding. (Col. 1:9)
272. I am able to walk worthy of the Lord, fully pleasing to Him. (Col. 1:10)
273. I choose to be fruitful in every good work, increasing in the knowledge of God. (Col. 1:10)
274. I am able to be strengthened with all might, according to His glorious power, for all patience and longsuffering, and joy. (Col. 1:11)
275. I have been delivered from the powers of darkness. (Col. 1:13)
276. I have been translated into the kingdom of Jesus Christ. (Col. 1:13)
277. I have redemption through His blood, the forgiveness of sins. (Col. 1:14)
278. I am indwelt by Him in whom all fulness dwells. (Col. 1:19,27)
279. I now work according to His working which works in me mightily. (Col. 1:29)

280. As I have received Him, so I can walk in Him. (Col. 2:6)
281. I am able to be rooted and built up in Him, abounding in thanksgiving. (Col. 2:7)
282. I am complete in Him. (Col. 2:10)
283. Every power in the universe is subject to Him and I am in Him. (Col. 2:10)
284. I have been buried through baptism and raised through faith in the power of God who raised Him from the dead. (Col. 2:12)
285. He has dismissed all evidence against me, taking it out of the way, nailing it to the cross. (Col. 2:14)
286. In my behalf he disarmed principalities and powers, making a public spectacle of them through the cross. (Col. 2:15)
287. Being raised with Christ I now seek those things which are above, where Christ is sitting. (Col. 3:1)
288. I choose to set my mind on things above and not on things on the earth. (Col. 3:2)
289. I died and my life is hid with Christ in God. (Col. 3:3)
290. Christ is my life. (Col. 3:4)
291. When He appears I shall appear with Him in glory. (Col. 3:4)
292. I choose to do everything in the name of the Lord Jesus, giving thanks to God. (Col. 3:17)
293. I choose to do everything heartily as unto the Lord. (Col. 3:23)
294. I know that from Him I shall receive the reward. (Col. 3:24)
295. My sanctification is the will of God. (1 Thess. 4:3)
296. God has called me to holiness. (Thess. 4:7)
297. If I die, my spirit will come with Jesus when He comes. (1 Thess. 4:14)
298. If I am alive when He comes, I will be caught up. (1 Thess. 4:17)
299. I am a son of light and not of darkness. (1 Thess. 5:5)

300. God has not appointed me to wrath but to obtain salvation. (1 Thess. 5:9)
301. The God of peace will sanctify me wholly. (1 Thess. 5:23)
302. My whole spirit, soul, and body will be preserved blameless unto the coming of Christ. (1 Thess. 5:23)
303. God is faithful who will see to it. (1 Thess. 5:24)
304. God chose me for salvation from the beginning. (2 Thess. 2:13)
305. I was called by the gospel to obtain the glory of Jesus, my Lord. (2 Thess. 2:14)
306. He has loved me and given me everlasting consolation and good hope by grace. (2 Thess. 2:16)
307. God and Jesus will comfort my heart. (2 Thess. 2:17)
308. They will also establish me in every good word and work. (2 Thess. 2:17)
309. The word of the Lord will have free course in me and be glorified. (2 Thess. 3:1)
310. I will be delivered from unreasonable and wicked men. (2 Thess. 3:2)
311. God is faithful who will establish me and will guard me from the evil one. (2 Thess. 3:3)
312. God is directing my heart into His love and into the patience of Christ. (2 Thess. 3:5)
313. God has not given me a spirit of fear, but one of love, power, and soundness of mind. (1 Tim. 1:9)
314. He has saved and called me with a holy calling which He has given me in Christ. (2 Tim. 1:9)
315. I know whom I have believed and know that He is able to keep what I have committed to Him. (2 Tim. 1:12)
316. The scriptures have been given that I may be complete, furnished to every good work. (2 Tim. 3:17)
317. The Lord will deliver me from every evil work and preserve me for His heavenly kingdom. (2 Tim. 4:18)
318. The grace of God that brings salvation has appeared to

me, teaching me to live soberly, righteously, and godly in this age. (Titus 2:11-12)

319. He gave Himself for me that he might redeem me from wickedness. (Titus 2:14)
320. He also died and rose to make me His pure one, marked out as His own, eager to do good. (Titus 2:14)
321. He has saved me according to His mercy, by the washing of regeneration and the renewing of the Holy Spirit. (Titus 3:5)
322. He has poured out His Spirit on me abundantly through Jesus. (Titus 3:6)
323. I have been justified by His grace and have become an heir according to the hope of eternal life. (Titus 3:7)
324. The sharing of my faith becomes effective by the acknowledging of every good thing that is in me in Jesus Christ. (Philemon 6)
325. I have continuous assistance from ministering spirits sent forth to minister to all the saved. (Heb. 1:14)
326. Because I am sanctified and am one with the Sanctifier, He is not ashamed to call me brother. (Heb. 2:11)
327. I my behalf Jesus broke the power of Him who has the power of death. (Heb. 2:14-15)
328. He also delivered me from the fear of death and all bondage connected to it. (Heb. 2:14-15)
329. I am a part of His house, holding fast the confidence and rejoicing in firm hope to the end. (Heb. 3:6)
330. I have become a partaker of Christ. (Heb. 3:14)
331. I have a promise of entering into His rest. (Heb. 4:1)
332. I have a right to come before the throne of grace to find mercy and obtain grace. (Heb. 4:16)
333. God's unchanging nature is an anchor to the soul both steadfast and sure. (Heb. 6:18-19)
334. I am saved to the uttermost because I have come unto God by Jesus. (Heb. 7:25)
335. Jesus is continuously making intercessions for me. (Heb. 7:25)

336. Jesus has entered into heaven itself, now to appear in the presence of God for me. (Heb. 9:24)
337. I have boldness to enter the holy of holies through His blood and have a true heart in full assurance of faith, cleansed from an evil conscience. (Heb. 10:19-22)
338. I am not one of those who draw back to perdition but of those who believe to the saving of the soul. (Heb. 10:39)
339. By faith I understand that the worlds were framed by the Word of God. (Heb. 11:3)
340. I look unto Jesus, the Author and Finisher of my faith. (Heb. 12:1-2)
341. I can escape discouragement, considering Him who endured so much for me. (Heb. 12:3)
342. If He chastens me it simply proves that I am His own and He loves me, doing it for my profit. (Heb. 12:7-11)
343. After discipline I will receive the peaceable fruit of righteousness. (Heb. 12:11)
344. I have received a Kingdom which cannot be moved and will serve God with reverence and godly fear. (Heb. 12:28)
345. He will never, never, never leave me. (Heb. 13:5-6)
346. Therefore I may boldly say, "The Lord is my Helper; I will not fear what man can do to me." (Heb. 13:6)
347. I have no continuing city, seeking one to come. (Heb. 13:14)
348. Therefore I will offer the sacrifice of praise, the fruit of the lips, giving thanks to His name. (Heb. 13:15)
350. I am being made complete in every good thing, God working in me every good thing which is well-pleasing in His sight. (Heb. 13:20-21)
351. I count it all joy when I fall into various kinds of trouble because I know that the testing of my faith produces patience. (James 1:2-4)
352. Patience works toward my completeness and maturity. (James 1:4)

353. As I lack wisdom, I ask it of God, who gives it to me and does not chide. (James 1:5)
354. I have been born to a living hope by the resurrection of Jesus Christ. (1 Pet. 1:3-4)
355. I am kept by the power of God through faith unto salvation. (1 Pet. 1:5)
356. The trial of my faith is more precious than gold. (1 Pet. 2:5)
357. I, as one of the living stones, am built up as a spiritual house and a holy priesthood to offer up spiritual sacrifices acceptable to God. (1 Pet. 2:5)
358. I am a part of a chosen generation, a royal priesthood, a holy nation, a peculiar people that I may show forth His praises. (1 Pet. 2:9)
359. I may cast all my care upon Him because He cares for me. (1 Pet. 5:7)
360. His divine power has given unto me all things that pertain to life and godliness. (2 Pet. 1:3)
361. I, according to His promise, look for a new heaven and a new earth, wherein dwelleth righteousness. (2 Pet. 3:13)
362. When I sin I have an advocate, Jesus Christ the Righteous. (1 John 2:1)
363. The anointing I have received from Him abides in me and teaches me concerning all things. (1 John 2:27)
364. I am a child of God now; it does not appear what I shall be, but this I know: that when he appears, I shall be like him for I shall see Him as he is. (1 John 3:2)
365. I have been born of God and have overcome the world; this is the victory that overcomes the world, even our faith. Greater is He that is in me than he that is in the world. (1 John 4:4; 5:4)

THESE ARE CONFESSIONS OF
GOD'S NEW CREATIONS!

Notes

Chapter 2

1. Charles Haddon Spurgeon, *The New Park Street Pulpit # 277,* p. 417.

2. Ibid.

3. Andrew Murray, *The Two Covenants* (Fort Washington, PA: Christian Literature Crusade, 1974), p. 2.

Chapter 3

1. Malcolm Smith, *Blood Brothers in Christ* (Old Tappan, NJ: Fleming H. Revell Co., 1975), p. 14.

2. Murray, Ibid., p. ix.

3. Clay Trumbull, *The Blood Covenant* (Kirkwood, MO: Impact Books, 1975), p. 4.

Chapter 4

1. Tract, *The Baptist Faith and Message* (Nashville, TN: The Sunday School Board of the Southern Baptist Convention, 1963), p. 7.

2. Trumbull, Ibid., p. 85.

3. Ibid., p. 87.

4. Ibid., p. 89.

5. Ibid., p. 90.

6. Ibid., p. 93.

7. Ibid., p. 94.

8. Ibid., Appendix, p. 25.

Chapter 5

1. Spurgeon, Ibid., pp. 419-420.

Chapter 6

1. W. E. Vines, *Expositional Dictionary of New Testament Words* (Westwood, NJ: Fleming H. Revell Co., 1940), p. 54.

2. Ibid., p. 97.

3. Murray, Ibid., p. 101.

4. E. W. Kenyon, *The Blood Covenant* (Seattle, WA: Kenyon's Gospel Publishing Co., 1969), p. 71.

Chapter 7

1. W. H. Griffith Thomas, *Christianity Is Christ* (Chicago, IL: Moody Press, 1965), p. 5.

2. Ian Thomas, *The Saving Life of Christ* (Grands Rapids, MI: Zondervan Publishing Co., 1961), p. 19.

3. S. D. Gordon, *In Christ* (Grand Rapids, MI: Baker Book House, 1964), p. 10.

4. F. J. Huegel, *Bone of His Bone* (Grand Rapids, MI: Zondervan Publishing Co., 1962), p. 13.

Chapter 8

1. Vines, Ibid., p. 292

Chapter 9

1. Fritz Reinecker and Cleon Rogers, *The Linguistic Key to the Greek New Testament* (Grand Rapids, MI: Zondervan Publishing Co., 1976), p. 367.
2. John Murray, *Redemption Accomplished and Applied* (William B. Eerdman's Publishing Co., 1955), p. 128.
3. Andrew Murray, Ibid., p. 96.
4. Ibid., p. 124.

Chapter 10

1. Paul Billheimer, *The Universe Is Romantic* (Unpublished notes given to JRT by Billheimer).

Chapter 12

1. Nathan Stone, *The Names of God* (Chicago, IL: Moody Press, 1944), pp. 125-126.
2. Ibid., p. 127.
3. Vines, Ibid., p. 298.
4. Ibid., p. 284.
5. E. W. Kenyon, *Two Kinds of Life* (Lynnwood, WA: Kenyon's Gospel Publishing Society, 1971), p. 59.
6. E. W. Kenyon, *The Father and His Family* (Lynnwood, WA: Kenyon's Gospel Publishing Society, 1971), p. 218.

Chapter 13

1. Reinecker and Rogers, Ibid., p. 769.
2. Vines, Ibid., p. 167.

Chapter 14

1. Andrew Murray, *The Master's Indwelling* (Alexandria, LA: Lamplighter Publications, n. d.), p. 72.
2. Ruth Paxson, *Rivers of Living Waters* (Chicago, IL: Moody Press, 1930), pp. 70-71.

Chapter 15

1. Watchman Nee, *The Glorious Church* (Tapei, Taiwan: The Gospel Book Room, 1968), p. 20.